S. JAMES MEYER

Living *with* Real Presence

Eucharist AS AN APPROACH TO *life*

TWENTY-THIRD PUBLICATIONS

twentythirdpublications.com

Theological Reductionism - PP 28-9

Listening to Understand Rather Than
~~Listen Only~~ to Respond - P.40

"Sore-Ish" P 41

Jesus Did Church Where ever there
were People 66

P. 68 - Me ~~affect~~ affect others

P.~~80~~ 81 - Differences = Whole

P 90 - 3 IMAGES of God

P. 111 - All Encompassing Love = Real
Eucharist

P. 115 → Chapter 3.5 Eucharist
as All Relationships

To all God's people,
all the time.
Blessed are we
who have been
called to share
in this meal.

TWENTY-THIRD PUBLICATIONS
977 Hartford Turnpike Unit A
Waterford, CT 06385
(860) 437-3012 or (800) 321-0411
www.twentythirdpublications.com

Cover photo: stock.adobe.com / Love You Stock

ISBN: 978-1-62785-718-5
Printed in the U.S.A.

 A division of Bayard, Inc.

CONTENTS

FIRST, A STORY

We gathered around the island in my mom's kitchen. Someone made popcorn, and my brother emerged from the basement with an armload of cold Pabst Blue Ribbon beers, which he brought specifically for this occasion. We had just returned from the wake service honoring my grandfather, and what better tribute could we, his progeny, offer than to gather in his memory, share the beer he served at the card table in his own home, and tell stories. This is how he lived and loved, surrounded by family, laughing, talking, and simply being present with one another.

Each of us, we discovered, knew Grandpa uniquely. Our lives had been affected in different and individual ways by what he said, how he related, and the way he lived. For the first time, I saw him through my dad's eyes, and I could see how my father and his father were one. Likewise, I discovered Grandpa through the eyes and heart of my mother, who entered the family at the age of twenty, and through my sisters and my brother. Individually, we knew him only partially. But in shared communion with each other, we could know him far more completely.

We shared the moral code he passed to us, including his commitment to a life of purpose, his insistence on integrity, his devotion to family, and his instruction to always be your brother's keeper.

As the evening grew late, it became increasingly obvious to me that Grandpa was present with us in that kitchen. He lived and breathed in us, around us, among us, and between us in a very real way. He was one in us, and we were one with him. This is how love works.

When we think of real presence in Eucharist, we tend to forget that presence is not a thing; it is an experience, an encounter, and a real form of intimacy. If we dare go deep in our spirituality, we discover that real presence is a way of life, perhaps *the* way of life that brings hope, compassion, peace, harmony, mercy, joy, and love to us, to our relationships, and to all humanity. It is the source of all happiness now and forever.

Part One

As Real
as It Gets

JUMPING
WITH REAL JOY

I come from a line of rural and semi-rural German Catholics for whom everything, including Mass on Sunday, was a chance to get together, laugh out loud, and play a little Sheepshead. In fairness, this doesn't mean we didn't take our faith seriously. Quite to the contrary. I have never known a community of people who truly understood how to integrate life and faith like those folks did. Gathering for Mass was not about stepping aside from life; it was about connecting in life. We brought ourselves, our real selves, sometimes even our real smells, into communion with each other.

From that perspective, either church wasn't sacred, or all of life was sacred. Either church wasn't a place for reverence, or all of creation was a place for reverence. I was raised to believe it was the latter. Church and life were entangled like family dinners and laughter, like pot roast and potatoes. I couldn't really tell where one stopped and the other started.

On a particularly sweltering Saturday evening in August, we gathered for Mass at Corpus Christi Catholic Church, a small country parish perched on a hill in Bakerville, Wisconsin. It was admittedly a bit cliché, a scene at sunset amidst rolling cornfields, the parish cemetery across the road, and a local country tavern—Jerome's Country Bumpkin—just down the hill, where two quarters dropped on the pine bar would buy an eight-ounce glass of Pabst Blue Ribbon for yourself and a second for whoever was standing alongside you.

If you've ever been to Wisconsin in early August, you already know how the weather will curl your hair. On this particular evening, the humidity hung so thick your glasses steamed, and the mosquitoes were so hungry they lifted livestock out of the surrounding pastures. Our church was without air conditioning because, after all, we were of rugged rural stock. We had no use for the energy-guzzling, air-polluting, soft comforts needed in the city. The cabs on the tractors were a different matter, of course.

Inside the church, Father Charlie told the acolytes to serve Mass in their street clothes, while he vested only in an alb and stole sans chasuble. "There is nothing holy about heat stroke," he told the community. He brought a pragmatic and approachable disposition to liturgy that some might find borderline scandalous by today's standards. Say what you will about his style, but the church was full that evening and the people were happy. With electric fans whirring in every corner and overhead, the women waved worship aids in front of their faces and the men, strong and stoic farmers, pretended to be unaffected even as they discreetly wiped their brows with handkerchiefs.

Making his way down the side aisle, Kenny Stumpfenbach stopped to open the window near where we were seated. These were tilt-style stained glass windows with a latch halfway up. By unhitching the latch and pulling it inward, the bottom of the window tilted outward. It was a very functional design for a man of average height. But Kenny lived on the upswing of life's bell curve, so the latch remained a couple inches above his upstretched arm, which, as a side note, bore the inevitable stain of failed antiperspirant. With one hand braced against the wall to steady himself, he rose onto his tiptoes. At the very peak of his pirouette, his reach still fell a bit short of the latch. Determined, Kenny jumped. It was a bit comical to watch this stout man push all his heft into a hop that raised his heels no more than a two-by-four on edge. Then he jumped again. And again. And yet again. With each leap and swing of his hock-like arm, a large ring of keys socialized with the loose coins in his pocket. And with each landing, the gravity of their force pulled his trousers down about a half inch. And then another half inch. And another.

To my brother and me, this was just about the funniest thing we could imagine happening in church. Raised to be at least marginally proper, we restrained our laughter. At first. Then we made eye contact. It started as a silent chuckle, escalated to repressed chortles, and erupted in convulsive giggles that shook our bodies. My eyes watered like open hydrants, and I bit into the heel of my hand to hold back audible guffaws. Each time I thought I had it under control, I'd hear a snort leak from my brother and the cycle would start over.

Before you rush to judge us for laughing at poor Mr. Stumpfenbach, please realize we were a rather small and tight community. We knew the whole extended Stumpfenbach clan, went to school with Kenny's kids and their cousins, and knew where they all lived. Likewise, they knew all of us. They wrote "wash me, I'm dirty" in the dust on the back window of my dad's Mercury, and they brought my parents banana bread when I was in the hospital after brain surgery. We weren't laughing at Kenny in a cruel way, we were delighting in the ridiculousness of the whole scene as one does with close family and friends. And it was ridiculous! Here was a middle-aged man launching himself into a mid-Mass latch leap with such vigor he was jumping out of his pants. How can you not delight in such a magnificent and poetic expression of the human condition? This is humanity created in God's own image and likeness. And, dang, it's beautiful!

This was a community gathered for Eucharist. And it was authentically human. And it was joy-filled. There was a real presence of peace and calm, a real presence of community and communion. Life was hard for a lot of these folks, but they leaned into it together. They laughed together. They lived and loved together. During good times and bad, there was always joy. Through births and baptisms, divorces and deaths, there was always joy. Even in the absence of happiness, there remained an abiding joy.

As people leave church today, they'll often remark that a story in the homily was so funny they wanted to laugh out loud, or that the message was so poignant they wanted to break into applause. "Why didn't you?" I ask. "Why didn't you express your delight and joy?" They typically look back at me oddly perplexed, as though the answer is obvious to everyone else. I wait. Inevitably, they explain with the quasi-hushed tone of a mother correcting a child, "Well, I just didn't think it was appropriate in church."

Not appropriate to express human joy at Mass?! Not appropriate to express human joy when gathered in communion as one body?! Who decided that? It's bizarre. On the way into church, people are upbeat, smiling, ready with a quick wit and friendly banter. They're mostly authentic, bringing a real presence through the door. Likewise on the way out. But as soon as they step into the nave, it's as though they're waiting in line at the DMV. Faces turn to stone. What's that about?

When I recently used the term "Catholic joy" in conversation with my wife...

Before going on, I should pause here and introduce you to Michelle. She is as down-to-earth, feet-on-the-ground, anchored-in-reality as the roots of an apple tree. When we go biking, she avoids paved trails, preferring crushed granite and dirt trails because they're closer to the earth and more natural. On a hot day, she'd rather walk in the woods than sit by a pool. Early in our relationship, she resisted microwave ovens because they sacrifice authenticity for speed. I was young and shallow, so I didn't even understand what she was talking about, but you get the picture. I met Michelle in the 1980s, an era when everything from music to color, from eyelashes to personalities, was synthetic, and I fell in love with how real she was. She brought a real presence to a manufactured world. In her real presence, her deep appreciation for trilliums and heavy quilts and good books, she showed me the centered peacefulness of joy. She showed me how joy isn't something we get from life, it's the expression a grateful, loving heart gives to life. And it's contagious. When you express your joy into the world, the winds of spirit blow joy seeds into all open hearts around you.

Back on topic: when I recently used the term "Catholic joy" in conversation with my wife, her immediate response was, "That's an oxymoron." Let's not just brush over that. Here's a woman who was raised and confirmed in the Church, got married to me in the Church, brought three children for baptism and First Communion in the Church, and watched her oldest son get married in the Church; so many of her most joyful life experiences have been embedded in the Church—and yet she finds the term *Catholic joy* to be self-contradicting.

When she told me this, I got up from my chair and poured more wine into my glass. We were going to be there a while and the conversation promised to be fascinating. By the way, we greatly under-emphasize the importance of good conversation during marriage preparation. I have grown to believe the deep listening, sharing, and discovery that happens in meaningful conversation between spouses is a brilliant form of mutual prayer. When entered in loving openness with your partner, it is every bit as much of a spiritual encounter and "God experience" as any prayerful practice there is. I wanted to know more—understand more—about Michelle's experience.

She went on to explain how, starting as far back into her childhood as she could remember, she was told not to be her real self in church. Don't slouch, don't fidget, don't talk. Be quiet, be humble, be pure. Hide your sins, hide your secrets, hide your body. You shouldn't look that way. You shouldn't think that way. You certainly shouldn't dress that way. The message throughout her childhood and adolescence was clear and consistent: You're not good enough as you are. You are not acceptable and presentable as you are. Rise above your humanity and become more like Jesus, but don't think you can be like Jesus—he's the Son of God, and you're a sinner.

Yikes. Where is the joy in all that? Where is the Eucharist in all that? Where is real presence in all that?

Three things here: 1) We send mixed messages about authenticity to our children. On one hand, we say God made them and loves them just as they are, but on the other hand, we tell them they're sinners and need to rise above their human condition. It's a paradox that most adults, much less teenagers, can't reconcile, so we spend a lifetime either trying to escape our true nature or abandoning religion. The only other option, which many end up choosing, is to live with dissonance and disharmony. How can we ever hope to be in communion with God and with one another when we live in disunion within ourselves? 2) Real presence means authentic presence, not put-on-a-false-front presence. The whole point of Christmas and incarnation, the very reason Jesus came to live among us, and why it matters that he infuses the Eucharist with his own real presence, is to illustrate once and for all that God

11

seeks to be with us as we are, meeting us wherever we are, and walking alongside us as we journey forward in love. That's all very joyful! Right? I mean that *is* the Good News. 3) How can we enter real presence with Christ when real presence with our selves eludes us? You can't engage real presence with another, even when the other is Christ, if you are disguising or denying your own authentic self.

Most of us will accept without argument that you cannot enter authentic love if you're not free to be yourself. We need to be authentically present to it to be fully in it. This is where and how love flourishes. A baby of socially dubious parentage born in a remote barn among stinky animals and smelly shepherds—that's reality, and that's love. A couple of fishermen fresh off the boat, unbathed, uncultured, and slow on the uptake—that's as real as life gets, and that's who Jesus chose as his apostles. A lone Samaritan woman drawing water from a community well—that's where we learn what real presence looks like. I wonder how many of these people would feel welcome in our churches.

The gift of Eucharist liberates us to encounter Christ's real presence with our own: Here I am—broken, bleeding, and poured out for you. Here I am—flesh, blood, sweat, and tears openly shared with you. Here I am—hopes, dreams, anxieties, and a sleepless night offered all for you.

Here *I am that I am*
loving who *you are that you are.*

It's beautiful. It's real. And it's the most joyful gift imaginable. How can we resist eating that up? How can we resist drinking that in?

Somehow in our quest to get closer to Christ—closer to the divine—we have felt it necessary to distance ourselves from our own humanity. How utterly absurd is that?! Mrs. Hyde, who taught religion to us in the ninth grade, told us we need to meet Jesus halfway. Yes, she explained, God comes to us on earth through Jesus, but we can't expect him to walk all the way to the detention room with us. If we mess up, if we skip class or lust after girls, we're on our own. My friend, Paul, raised his hand and asked if that applies to the really big sins like violating the dress code and chewing gum in the library. She told him not to get smart. But the whole conversation left me with two questions: What good is a God who won't come with me to the detention room? And where did this woman study theology?

All of this pettiness undermines the very foundations of our creed, standing contrary to everything we profess to believe. As creator, God creates humanity in God's own image and likeness. We don't hang signs at the church entrance telling people to check their humanness at the door. God manifested as Jesus Christ takes on the totality of our humanity. It's what incarnation is all about. Why would we repress that at Mass? God manifested as Holy Spirit ignites our human form with divine gifts. Why on earth would we seek to transcend that form when gathered for Eucharist? The misguided notion that God and godliness is separate from humanity and humanness has corrupted our understanding of and appreciation for church, religion, Christian spirituality, and even the Body of Christ. We have lost so much by perpetuating the distance Jesus came to bridge.

Have you ever been greeted by someone who was so excited to see you their eyes popped, their smile beamed, and they lost all sense of propriety? I once flew home after a business trip and looked forward to being met at the airport by Michelle and Jacob, who was four at the time. But there were thunderstorms, flight delays, and cancellations. I was supposed to arrive at 6:00 pm, but it was going on midnight before I finally emerged from the jet bridge. Exhausted, bleary-eyed, and expecting to catch a taxi home, I heard a child's voice power above the crowd: "There's my daddy!" And this small boy—my son in whom I am well pleased—exploded through the legs of strangers, his prized Milwaukee Brewers cap glued to his head, and he sprang with great excitement into my arms. That's joy. That's reverence. That's love. And that, dare I say, is real presence. If we do not recognize and celebrate the living Body of Christ in moments such a this, how can we expect people to recognize and celebrate Holy Communion in the too-often starched context of Mass?

Fruit of Our Labor. Work of Our Hands.

J udy Meyer bent at the knees and hoisted the thick
wooden breadboard onto the kitchen table. Still in
her mid-thirties, she was young enough to imagine
the romance of a starlit boat ride on the Seine and the
glamor of an inaugural ball, but elegance would have to
wait for another day. Or perhaps another life. She plopped
the dough on the board and began to work it with her
skilled and experienced hands. Good things were about to
happen. Life was right after all. In this corner of the world,
in this household on East Ninth Street, money was tight,
but at least the hungry would get fed.

The breadboard itself was notable. A large slab of
hardwood an inch and a half thick, it was sprinkled with
water, christened with oils, and dusted with flour. For a

slight woman who measured two inches beyond five feet only because she poofed her hair, moving it from cabinet to table required conviction. Eventually, she would call on one of her preteen sons to set up the makeshift altar, not because she couldn't, but rather because it fostered a sense of emerging capacity in the boy. "We learn by doing," she would teach him. Nonetheless, it was a symbiotic arrangement. The son gained a growing sense of capability and contribution, while the mother gained freedom from the chore.

In addition to baking all her own bread, my mother made nearly everything we ate. From the jelly on our breakfast toast to the cakes served at family weddings, if it went into our bellies, it likely came from her kitchen—the fruit of her labor and the work of her hands. As a young boy in a time when gender roles were expected and unquestioned, I found it curious that we'd go to Mass and a man, not a woman, was standing at the table in a gown preparing the meal. The first and best priest I knew, the one I loved most—the priest who read us stories, compassionately preached to us about character and morality, broke our bread, and consecrated our lives—was a woman.

Our home was under constant renovation, an ongoing project of innovation and improvement—like life itself, I suppose. My dad would sit in his recliner on Sunday with a large drawing board and T-square, and within a week a wall somewhere in the house would be missing. The bed I slept in, the bathroom I showered in, and the table we gathered around for dinner—the same table on which my mother would place the large breadboard and knead the dough—were all the fruits of his labor and the work of his hands. Decades later, when I sit on a stool in my own workshop using some of the same tools he used and running my hand over freshly sanded oak, I still channel his discerning craftsmanship and patient mentorship. I do it in memory of him albeit of a far lesser quality.

So when Sister Mary Alice prepared us as second graders for First Communion, the whole narrative made sense to me. It fit into my frame of reference. Jesus, like me, was raised as a carpenter's son. His mother, I imagined, baked the bread, cookies, and pot roast they ate. It made sense to the eight-year-old me that he would gather around a table with his friends, break the bread, pour the wine, and share it. That's what people who love each other do. And, of course he would say, "Do this in memory of me." Again, in my experience at least, that's what people who love each other did. The people I loved gathered around a table and broke bread together to celebrate birthdays, anniversaries, baptisms, weddings, and funerals. This is how we raised each other up and consecrated the life we shared. It's also how we celebrated ordinary daily living in the community of family. In fact, it was a way of life—a way of an anchored and enriching life filled with love, laughter, and joy, even as I romanticize it in retrospect.

We were not a perfect family by any means. I was constantly in trouble for shirking my responsibilities and lying about it to my father, who had neither patience for laziness nor tolerance for deceit. Somehow, he forgave me over and over. I guess that's what love does. I griped relentlessly about some of the meals my mother prepared, especially the corn hotdish with the stewed tomatoes—a phenomenon I cannot explain to this day. My mother worked tirelessly to feed a growing family on a carpenter's paycheck, yet I was perpetually ungrateful and openly critical of the things I didn't like. Somehow, she forgave me over and over. Again, I guess that's what love does.

As in so many other Catholic households, a copy of DaVinci's *Last Supper* hung in a gilded frame in our dining room. What they did in that painting, we did around our table; what we did, they did. There was a certain cohesion to the whole happening. Religion, family, dinner, Eucharist, faith, science, sacraments, math homework, picking raspberries, pounding nails—it all blended in texture and flavor like a good chili on a cold day.

At the center of it all, anchoring and connecting the whole shebang, was love. But it was a gritty love, not the tidy, saccharine love of a Hallmark Channel Christmas movie. Sometimes my parents argued, especially when dad would invite the neighbors over to play cards without first consulting mom. In my mom's mind, it was impossible to play Pinochle without first cleaning the entire house and making a chocolate torte—if we're gathering people around our table even if it's just to play cards, we need newly-baked bread of some sort to break and share. And sometimes, almost daily actually, my siblings and I fought. We fought about who's turn it was to do the dishes (not mine), who should get the last piece of pizza (me), who was bugging who (jury's still out), and who started it (never me, of course). Voices were raised and doors were slammed. And sometimes my parents lost their patience with us. Fair enough.

Love, I learned, is messy. People, even people you love, will take you for granted, say hurtful things to you or about you, pass judgment upon you, take advantage of you, maybe even cheat you (it really was NOT my turn to wash those damn dishes). Most often, at least in healthy relationships, they don't intend to hurt us or wrong us. They're just so preoccupied with their own self-interest in the moment that they didn't really consider the impact on us. Forgive them for they know not what they are doing. In fairness, we likewise trip over our own small-mindedness and do it to them too. (Actually, it might have been my turn to do the dishes. Maybe. Well, probably.) Honesty, humility, and objectivity demand we admit this. Otherwise, we're living a lie while pretending to pursue truth. Perhaps one of the most restorative things we can do is self-admit our capacity to be annoying and even hurtful. This is one of the great gifts offered inadvertently by teenagers—they unwittingly remind their parents that unconditional love demands we forgive each other for being annoying.

In our minds of course, we create some impressive contortions of logic to justify our own missteps and misspeaks. We protect our egos by finding or inventing ways to justify the pain we inflict upon people and relationships. Think about it. Honestly. We exaggerate the splinters in our neighbor's eye while convincing ourselves that the planks in our own eye are formed of polished Italian marble that has been blessed by the pope himself.

But none of that nonsense is bigger than love. It happens because we're all still growing. We're all fractured and only partially baked. None of us is complete. This is why we need reconciliation, mercy, and forgiveness. It's also why we need a penitential rite (here I am, as I am, imperfections and all—Lord have mercy!), a sign of peace, and Holy Communion. We need all these things not only as ritual, but as attitude, action, instruction, inclusion, and inspiration. And we need them not merely for an hour on Sunday morning but as a way of life every moment of every day.

You've been very patient as I've self-indulged my own frame of reference. Here's the point I've been illustrating: if our experience of Eucharist does not reflect our actual life experience, then we either are being disingenuous about Eucharist or dishonest about our life. Or both.

Admittedly, that's a big, hairy, audacious statement. Maybe you want to take a few minutes, stir a little Irish crème into your coffee, and figure out what you want to do with it.

Sometimes I wonder if we struggle to understand Eucharist in church because we don't first open ourselves to eucharist in the world. If we close ourselves to the basic humanity in one another, how will we ever see the divinity in bread and wine?

Sometimes all you have to do is show up, reach out to someone in need, and Boom! just like that the real presence of Christ shows up among us. We get to participate in meaningful transformation through eucharistic experiences. For example, on a street corner one night, I started talking to a guy named Lonzo who hadn't eaten in a couple of days. So I walked across the street to buy him a convenience store ham & cheese sandwich. It was far from heroic; it was merely human. It took very little effort on my part. In fact, all it really required of me was a willingness to be present to the needs of another human being and about five dollars, which is less than half a beer at a ballgame. Being Christ to others and seeing Christ in others isn't complicated.

Lonzo took it from me, ate it, and offered himself in return. He broke himself open, poured himself out, and shared his story with me. It was a blessed and sacred encounter that I ate up and drank in. We shared a very real and authentic presence with each other, a living Christ moment—*for where two or three are gathered in my name, there am I with them* (Mt 18:20).

When sitting around with a group of high school students, the conversation inevitably turned to testimony about why they don't attend Mass: It's boring. I don't get anything out of it. It's stupid. Everyone's a hypocrite. My parents don't like going anymore, either. They dumped out the entire bucket of tried and true critiques and criticisms at my feet.

I smiled and nodded.

This time, I didn't counter any of their points. I didn't seek to justify ritual, explain the value of community, or play any of the tired clichés about getting out of something what you put into it. I just sat and listened until they ran out of gas.

Then I asked a simple question, "Do you think it has to be that way?"

"No," they quickly responded.

"Can you think of a time, even one, where Mass wasn't boring and stupid? Can you recall ever having an experience at Mass which was meaningful and enriching, where you left feeling very glad you went."

Then the stories started to break open and pour out.

"At the end of a day I spent volunteering with my family."

"When I went to the funeral for my best friend's grandma. I was really glad to be there for him."

"When my dad started chemo. We brought him to a Mass where they were doing Anointing of the Sick and he was so grateful he cried. I had never seen him cry."

"After a really tough week when my sister attempted suicide."

You see the trend, right? Eucharist is so much more meaningful when we bring our own flesh and blood to it, when we bring the real presence of our own human experience of brokenness and vulnerability, when we come giving the fruit of our labors and the work of our hands, when we offer ourselves up in love for and with one another.

REAL DEEP

Isabella was a precocious four-year-old who asked a lot of questions and talked non-stop. Filled with life, optimism, and energy, she loved climbing onto her grandfather's lap with her favorite storybook about a family who travels through time together. Whenever her grandpa would ask, "Where is God?" Isabella's eyes would widen, she'd giggle a little, and she'd point right at his heart. She knew. She instinctively knew that love comes to life inside us; that God is immediately present to us, through us, within us, among us, around us, and between us. At the age of four, Isabella did not question or doubt the mystery of incarnation. She simply entered it and lived it fully and joyfully. What a gift! What an example!

Unfortunately, that was the last time she answered the question so insightfully. Because when asked again at the age of eight, "Where is God?" she pointed upward toward the sky. From inner cheer to astrosphere—that's a long way to travel in just four years, even for God. Somehow as we guide children through the critical self-awareness threshold that registers around the age of seven, we introduce the notion that the realm of God is distant and separate from us, that God is a distinct being, albeit a Supreme Being, who while loving, forgiving, protecting, and comforting, sits upon a throne in some place or dimension we call *heaven*, a place or state that exists apart from and outside of ourselves. It all seems so far away. And with it, the child ends up learning that God can be accessed and known mostly through magical words called *prayer* but rarely through lived experience.

When Isabella was asked again, at the age of twelve, "Where is God?" she shrugged her shoulders and ran off to play soccer. And when asked at sixteen, she spoke a bit derisively without even looking up from her phone, "I don't know if I believe in God." What happened? How did her formative years journey along a trajectory from rudimentary mysticism to distance to disengagement to disbelief and finally land at dismissal?

Here's a thought: western religions in general have a pattern of taking a very deep and profound spirituality, one that requires an entire lifetime to grow into, and dilute it down to a level a seven-year-old can understand. And then we never grow it back up.

Think of it as *theological reductionism*. I probably need to apologize for that. It's not in my nature to use words having a combined Scrabble score higher than my IQ. But the problem they describe is even bigger than the words themselves. Allow me to explain by way of analogy. I once observed a focus group in which a seemingly happy, well-adjusted participant said, "Heart surgery is no big deal. It's just plumbing and electricity, like fixing a sump pump." I would call this *cardiovascular reductionism*—reducing the complexities and intricacies of the cardiovascular system down to their lowest denominator. In fairness, is the *plumbing and electricity* reference helpful in understanding heart surgery? Perhaps, but only if you're in the second grade. By the time you're in the sixth grade, you're ready to learn about atriums and valves, and by the time you're in high school you're ready to learn about the aorta, pulmonary arteries, and integration with the nervous system.

In every other pursuit, we begin teaching at a rudimentary level and then continuously go deeper and deeper into the complexities, systems, and nuances. If you tell a medical student that heart surgery is just like fixing a sump pump, she'll stop coming to class and use the time to study other material. Or to catch up on sleep. She'll also likely send an abruptly worded letter to her medical school administration requesting a refund. It's worth noting that this is exactly what we want her to do. None of us, after all, wants to see a doctor who understands the human heart at the same level as a kid who still gets excited about a My Little Kitty backpack.

Yet, when it comes to religion, we still talk to fully grown, well-educated adults like they're eight-year-olds who are incapable of cutting their own pork chops or understanding that babies don't come from storks. Why do we do this? We simplify deep and profound spiritual truths to mere pablum and then wonder why no one listens. I once sat with a group of ordained deacons as our bishop gave us a forty-five-minute lecture on how to pray, talking to us like children needing to be told to sit up straight and keep our elbows off the table. I've also sat through countless homilies about Eucharist that provided about as much depth and substance as a McDonald's commercial.

Let's be upfront about something: the spiritual, life-giving reality we encounter, experience, and share through Holy Communion reaches deeper than the oceans and beyond the stars. None of us is capable of fully understanding the mystery in this lifetime. But we're all capable of entering the mystery and growing in its richness. I cannot grasp the entire mystery of love, but throughout my lifetime I've grown toward an ever-deeper understanding. At seventeen, I thought love was about romance, chocolates, and magic, but after thirty-five years of marriage I understand it's about a lifetime of joys and tears, hope and loss, growth and grief. That doesn't negate romance and chocolates, it just gives them a whole lot more meaning. Eucharist—life blessed, broken, poured out, and shared—is much the same way. Arguably, it's exactly the same way.

What we teach to First Communicants is akin to counting on your fingers, and it's a far cry from calculus. Think of it this way: you are not who you were when you were a child. The wholeness of you is now so much bigger and deeper. You are your thoughts, dreams, relationships, talents, and values; you are the love you share and the lives you touch. When we say we give our body and blood to something, to a purpose, a cause, or a relationship, we don't merely mean our physical bodies; we mean the substance and essence of our entire lives. When people reduce our *being* to our physical appearance, we feel dehumanized and objectified. Likewise, the Body and Blood of Christ is so much greater, so much deeper, and so much more encompassing than the mere objective physicality of Jesus' bodily flesh.

Theological reductionism is at the heart of the growing disconnect between religion and people, between Eucharist and humanity—a disconnect that is now at crisis level for the Church. Many in the Church, especially several members of the clergy, want to attribute the epidemic of religious disengagement to dark lures with names like materialism, consumerism, and liberalism. To this, I say malarkey. Nonsense. That would be a convenient explanation, but it's simply not true. That's like saying people avoid deep-fried brussels sprouts because they're lured away by romantic comedies.

People aren't staying away from Sunday Mass because they find shopping or soccer or Seinfeld reruns to be more enriching; they're staying away from Mass because they find cleaning their bathrooms to be more rewarding. Seriously, they'd rather help their moody middle-schooler figure out how to divide fractions. And for the record, that surly seventh grader would rather do her math homework than come to Mass. This has nothing to do with materialism.

I want to be clear about something here: I am not exaggerating. We live in a stressed-out, high-anxiety, tightly-wound, exhausted culture. Nearly everyone who isn't yet retired, and even many who are, live with unprecedented attention scarcity. They don't have enough time or energy to meet the demands and expectations of life.

For many, church just adds more demands and expectations without the depth to warrant the attention.

Now, hang on—I can sense you're running ahead of me, so let me catch up. Yes, a consistent, regular Sabbath practice could/should be the antidote to all this. As a culture, much of our stress has resulted from losing our collective spiritual moorings. Absolutely. We are people adrift. Taking a step back from all the crazy to celebrate Eucharist together could/should be the solution.

So why isn't it? Why don't people perceive it that way?

Let's refresh our coffee, scratch our chins, and talk honestly and openly about this. It's not as though all these people have never experienced church. My eighty-two-year-old mother, for example, who has always been a lifelong committed Catholic, now spends her Sunday mornings sewing quilts rather than going to Mass. That's not about consumerism or youth hockey tournaments. It's about theological reductionism.

Most people, my mother included, seek depth, meaning, insight, and connection, but not a superficial connection. They long for a profound connection with truth, love, and joy, which is exactly the sort of connection Eucharist could/should facilitate.

So why doesn't it? Why don't we experience it that way? Again, theological reductionism.

Oh my gosh, there is so much to unpack here. We reduce creation to a singular event at the dawn of time, reduce the brilliant truth of incarnation to Jesus' birthday, reduce the profound wholeness of Eucharist to a physical object, reduce the layered complexities of morality to mere behaviorism, and reduce the concept of heaven to a reward for good behavior like an eternal trip to Chuck E. Cheese. Oh wait, that would be hell.

I came from a place where the celebration of the Mass made sense to me. At least in theory, anyway. Yes, we were all broken, but we were pilgriming our way together toward wholeness. There was a recognition that we need each other, we need God, and we need to share our God-given gifts to nourish, sustain, and raise one another up. What didn't make sense to me then or now is the way we seemingly make the rules, structures, and rubrics wrapped around Eucharist more sacred and holy than the people sitting next to us.

Somehow along the way, I'm not sure when or how, the celebration of Eucharist became as much unlike a family dinner as you can imagine. We focus more on our posture than our relationships, and more about our physical presentation than our real presence.

Part Two

Substance
and Essence

THE HUMAN CONDITION

D r. Abramson looked more like a minor league batting coach than a professor of nineteenth-century British literature. He was a large-framed, burly guy who bought all his clothes at thrift stores and garage sales, where it was hard to find things that fit his build, so he settled for whatever was comfortable. But, boy, did that guy understand humanity.

When we finished discussing any novel, he'd ask us this question: "What does this say about the human condition?" It's a brilliant question and it applies equally well to *Pride and Prejudice* as it does to *Winnie-the-Pooh and the Honey Tree.*

It's an important question to ask of the Scripture stories passed to us through the generations. What does this say about the human condition? Sometimes, perhaps, we get too enamored by the religiosity of the gospels to remember that they are actually human stories about the human journey.

The story of the Last Supper is a great example. What happens if we dare to read it as literature? I understand that might make some people a little nervous but save your emails for a minute: I'm not suggesting we forget or dismiss that it's gospel, but rather that we allow ourselves to encounter it broadly as a human story rather than narrowly as a religious story. If we do this well and with earnest hearts, it won't diminish our understanding; it will expand it.

Exploring it in this way invites us to ponder motivation—why did Jesus do it? Why would he break the bread, proclaim "this is my body," and then pass it around the room? And the same with the cup—why would he take the cup of wine, proclaim "this is my blood" and then tell everyone to drink it? What commentary about the human condition does this story reveal?

Well, as anyone who has been in the role of a caregiver can attest, this is what love does. Call it human love, call it divine love: either way, Jesus tells us it's the same love. And when we love someone—I mean really love someone, such as a child screaming out in the middle of the night, a spouse in the advanced stages of a terrible disease, or an aging parent who might not even remember who we are, is this not what we're called to do, what we want to do—to break ourselves open and pour ourselves out?

When we're exhausted, beaten down, and at the end of our rope, isn't this still the body and blood of Christ we share with those we love? We break ourselves open and pour ourselves out because that's what love does.

When we love someone, we want to share the very substance and essence—the bread and wine—of our lives. So what does all this say about the human condition?

It says that love is willingly self-giving, that it moves us to give everything we are to those we love. And when we do this, when we do this in memory of Jesus himself, we become, in fact, one with one another and one with God. We become Eucharist.

Blessed, Broken, and Shared

"I want to talk to you about your homily. You said something that really bothers me." Jason was standing in the sacristy doorway, arms crossed, blocking anyone else's entrance or Fr. Ray's exit. In fairness, he didn't realize he was obstructing. Rather, like so many of us, he lingered obliviously in liminal space, either unable or unwilling to let go of the controllable comfort that held him. But self-comfort, especially when it's in the form of self-righteousness, is often little more than a wolf in sheep's clothing. It lures us into satisfaction and complacency before digging its teeth into our legs, thus preventing us from journeying into a deeper truth. Imagine a sprout, free of the seed casing, convinced the hard work is done and it's now fully grown, so it refuses to break through the topsoil into the sunlight. Of course, Jason didn't realize any of this; he wasn't aware that by coming only as far as the doorway he had made himself a poem. He just wanted to set the record straight with Father.

In many ways, we're all like that, aren't we? We have an incomplete understanding of God's great mysteries, but it's enough to give us security, and we don't want our boats rocked. We believe what we believe—and that's the end of it. But blind faith can be, well, blind. It can black out any new illumination. We never fully enter the welcoming light of a new room without exiting the controlled comfort of the room we're in. To create heart-space for new spiritual growth and discovery, we are always required to let go of something. Always. And that means being vulnerable. Yikes.

Growth also requires an admission from us—an admission that we are not yet whole, not yet complete. Ooh, this is often harder yet. It's comforting to believe we have life, death, and the afterlife all figured out; that somehow the five pounds of neurons and fats packed into our skulls have a grasp on infinite truth, or at least a close enough facsimile that we needn't keep traveling. How absurd is that, really? We spend the first thirty, forty, or fifty years of our lives wandering, stumbling, and tripping down a formative path rife with pain, confusion, and, sadly, often trauma. Finally, we take refuge on a spot where we can collect the pieces of our own truth and tape them together. It may be tenuous, but at least it makes sense, so we stay right there, holding it together. Although fragile, we feel whole for the first time. Or at least whole enough. We'd rather not move on and risk shaking things loose. If we are reminded of our brokenness, we might fall apart completely. So we cling. We cling to the tidy and simplistic understanding of Eucharist as taught to us when we were too young and innocent to recognize brokenness, much less cause it.

Then this Jesus shows up, the most whole and perfect person among us, and he doesn't even have to fake it. And what does he do? He breaks himself open and pours himself out. Shattered, vulnerable, bleeding, and hanging on a cross. "Do this in memory of me," he says. Holy smokes! That's a big ask. We tape the pieces of our lives together and try to pretend we're not broken; he breaks himself apart and distributes the pieces to all of us so that we have a chance to be whole for real with him. It's almost too much.

I've digressed, so let's get back to the story.... For Father Ray, Jason's words were triggering, taking him back to his early years in ministry, and to even earlier years to the relationship with his father, when in his insecurity, he perceived criticisms as threats. He took a deep breath and paused.

"Ok," he said. "Tell me more."

"You said we need to worry about our own heart before we tell others their actions are wrong." This was not actually what he had said, but it was a pretty good application of the message. Fr. Ray, or "Fray" as his friends called him, was impressed, so he simply nodded in agreement. He had found over the years that the healthiest way to encounter anyone—whether a surly staff member, a frustrated parishioner, or an upset neighbor—is by listening to

Listening to

understand rather than listening to respond. This is tough. When someone confronts us about things we've said or done, our first instinct is defensive. We want to protect our fragile, taped-together self-identity, so we listen for a crack in their argument and jab at it with a quick, debate-killing dagger. Let's shatter them before they shatter us. Personally, I'm still broken in this way, so it takes mindful discipline to set my ego aside, ignore the dialog in my own head, and objectively listen to what the other person is saying. Compassionate listening means vulnerability.

Leaning against the table, Fray tried to present himself as being comfortable and open to the conversation. For the most part, this was authentic albeit awkward. Previous conversations with Jason hadn't always gone well. Sometimes it felt to Fray like whenever he let a broken piece of himself fall to the table, people like Jason would pounce on it and hammer it into dust.

"We have a moral obligation to tell people when they're wrong," Jason continued. "This is why we've been given Catholic tongues—to correct the wrongful actions of others."

The words struck Fray as foreign. He had never heard the term *Catholic tongues* before, but he was quite confident Jason hadn't invented it.

"Huh. That's not really what the gospel says. It says we should pay more attention to the love that's inside our hearts, or not inside our hearts, before we go around telling other people what to do."

"No, that's wrong," Jason abruptly replied. "That's the part of your homily I have a big problem with."

Allow me to hit the pause button on this story for a moment. People often ask me if the stories I write about are true. Mostly, yes, they are. Sometimes I combine elements of a couple different stories to create one with more clarity and punch. And sometimes I add characters to give a story texture. Very often I change names, locations, and even ages and genders to protect identities. Overall, however, I adhere to the instruction of my Advanced Creative Writing Professor, Bruce Taylor, who insisted that good writers don't have to make things up, they just open their eyes. Real stories are happening around us all the time.

I think this is what Jesus did with his parables. Were the stories he told true? Well, sure-ish. More important, they were real. And that's what made them so relatable. They were extracted from the social and economic fabric of the time. Did the story of the good Samaritan really happen? As far as his listeners were concerned, it was a real-world story. What about the story of the prodigal son? Or the lost coin? Or the vineyard laborers? Again, yes, yes, and yes. Whether or not they represent factual reporting in a literal way is irrelevant. They convey timeless insights into human nature that help us even today as we seek a deeper understanding of how to live in loving wholeness with self, God, and others.

All that being said, the story we are in the midst of exploring is both true and real. I was there, listening and witnessing in the background as it unfolded. It's worth emphasizing this point because it's crazy. Seriously, it's off the chain. Here we had a very devout, churchgoing, late-middle-aged Catholic man arguing with his pastor about whether the gospel is right or wrong. The conversation wasn't about how to interpret or understand the gospel in light of its context, nor was it about how to apply it in our world today. It was about whether one of the foundational messages of the gospel is correct. I guess it's easier to dismiss or even deny Christ's teaching than to live up to its challenges. It's also easier to reduce Christ's teaching to a shallow level rather than deal with the complexities of depth.

We all know what Jason was doing in actuality. He was attempting to manipulate the gospel to support his personal ego narrative—that as a good Catholic he has The Truth and, therefore, he is morally obligated to go around telling everyone else they are wrong. "Don't bother me with the facts," my dad used to say with dry sarcasm, "I already have my opinion."

Let me be clear about two things: First, this is messed up. As Catholics, we are flawed pilgrims on a journey through life, doing our heartfelt best to love God and neighbor. We strive to be compassionate and merciful, and some days we're better at it than other days. We do not have it all figured out, but we're working on it. Now, in defense of Catholicism, we have two thousand years of theology, spirituality, and sacraments to illuminate the path, but we still stumble. We still get lost. Second, I'm not blaming Jason. I do it too. We all do it. Let's not kid ourselves. We slip our lives into an annotated Scripture at times, highlighting the parts that affirm us and ignoring or even crossing out the parts that challenge us. It's a lot more convenient that way.

In reality, we are all broken and, at least at times, we are all shattered, so we cuddle ourselves in the warm blanket of Scripture, pulling the soft parts close to our cheeks and folding the itchy parts away. This is all Jason was doing. He was folding away the scratchy part of the blanket. Who can blame him?

I owe you some context for this extended detour. Here's the point: Even though Eucharist is an experience we encounter and share again and again throughout our lives, our foundational understanding of it is decisively based in Scripture. We owe it to ourselves and to Christ to be careful that we have not snuggled into the cozy parts while folding away the itchy parts. Yes, there are itchy parts. Very itchy parts. More on that later. For now, back to our story....

Fray let Jason's desire to point out the splinter in his neighbor's eye linger in the air for a moment. The pause, the silence between the notes, is often the difference between music and noise. It can lend rhythm to dialog. He nodded and spoke, "You're saying the gospel is wrong?"

"Which gospel?" Jason asked as though he had lost his way in the convolutions of his own argument. Now, for your own future self-awareness, this rhetorical device is called the substitution heuristic. When we want to avoid an itchy question, we substitute a softer one. It's a convenient little ploy to go easy on ourselves. When my wife asks, "Have you cleaned the bathrooms yet?" I reply with, "What time do you want to leave for dinner?" See how I avoided an uncomfortable question I didn't want to answer by tossing out a softer question? In the Church, we avoid itchy questions such as, "How should we revere the Body of Christ alive in our world?" by substituting softer questions such as, "Can I eat an hour before receiving Communion?" Honestly, this is childish and inhibits spiritual growth. Another term for it is theological reductionism. We already discussed that.

Fray brought it back to the point, "The gospel we just proclaimed at Mass. Luke's gospel—the part about removing the big ol' beam from your own eye before pointing out the flaws in everyone else's. That's what you're saying you disagree with?"

"In your homily, you said we should focus on the love that's in our hearts, not on the sinful actions of other people."

"Yes. That's right."

"No, that's wrong. Father Chester says we have a moral obligation to correct our brothers. Our own hearts have nothing to do with it." Father Chester was a commentator on a fringe Catholic media outlet that is not actually sanctioned by the Church but is given more authority than the pope by its followers.

In the background, I washed and dried the eucharistic vessels a second time, finding an excuse to stay busy so I could continue eavesdropping. Was that wrong? Was my action dubious? Was my heart in the wrong place? My mind wandered to the teachings of St. Benedict—that we should treat all tools with the reverence we have for eucharistic vessels, and we should receive all people at our door as though we are receiving Christ himself. That can be so hard! Sometimes, I fear I'm a punk.

44

Fray was kind. He's not a punk. "If you have a loving heart, your speech and your actions will be loving. Your brother will see it by the loving way you live and by...."

Jason wasn't interested in pauses, silence between notes, and all that stuff. He jumped in, "But Father Chester says we must use our Catholic tongues to...."

Fray was human after all, too. His patience was waning. "I don't care what Father Chester says. I'm much more interested in what Jesus says. And Jesus says a good tree bears good fruit and a rotten tree bears rotten fruit. Tend the tree of your heart. That's what the gospel is saying. Do you think Jesus is wrong about that?"

Jason squirmed. What else could he do? I felt a little sorry for him. "Sometimes rotten fruit can be made good."

Fray softened. There was no need to drive this further and it was time to find common ground. I was impressed by how he turned it back toward a graced moment of spiritual growth. "Yes, water can be turned into wine. Lazarus can emerge from his tomb. That which is rotten can be made fresh again. But only by a heart that loves with the love of Christ. I'm not there yet. Neither are you or anyone else. And that's what Jesus says we need to focus on."

The apostles who gathered in the upper room with Jesus were not perfect either. Their hearts did not love with the love of Christ. Not yet at least. They tried, but they were broken and flawed just as we are. Even after following him for three years, hanging on his every word, they still struggled. They fought with each other over who was the greatest, who deserved a preferred seat at the table. They argued until Jesus said, "Get behind me, Satan."

Jesus knew this of course because he knew them. He washed their feet anyway. Just as he had with lepers, Samaritans, tax collectors, Pharisees, Wall Street bankers, homeless panhandlers, personal injury attorneys, Minnesota Vikings fans, and you and me, he loved them wholly. He sat at table, broke bread with them, and called them his best friends.

And since they (we) couldn't be like him, he became like them (us): broken.

Take a deep breath and let that fill your lungs with the fresh air of hope. Try listening to understand, not to respond. When my niece got sick with cancer while in high school, when the chemo caused her hair to fall out, her father and brother shaved their heads in solidarity. Why would they do such a thing? It wouldn't stop her hair from falling out. It wouldn't send the cancer into remission. So why? Because that's what love does. It was their way of breaking themselves open and pouring themselves out for her. Love goes to wherever the other person is, living beyond our own vanities and need for perfection.

This is what Jesus did.

We cheat ourselves when we think of Holy Communion apart from crucifixion and resurrection. Jesus instituted Eucharist on the very night he was betrayed and handed over. We celebrate this as part of our Holy Thursday/Good Friday/Easter Vigil liturgy. And we hang crucifixes in our sanctuaries and our homes. There is simply no way around it: brokenness—Jesus' and our own—is a central, inseparable theme of Eucharist. And, frankly, it's beautiful. It shows us just how unconditional love is.

This is a scratchy part of the blanket for a lot of Catholics, especially a segment among the super pious and devout. It's comforting to simply fold that back and reframe brokenness as something in our past rather than our present. My dear and valued friend, Msgr. Jim Dillenburg, once gave me this confusing compliment when my kids were ranging in age from about three to eleven: "I love how real your family is. When you come to Mass, your boys might look a little disheveled and they annoy each other in the pew. You and Michelle don't try to hide the truth about who you and they are, and I get the sense that the family you bring to Mass is the same family that gathers for dinner in your home." I wasn't sure how to take that, so he continued, "Christians have this habit of dressing their kids up for church, marching them in front of the priest with perfectly combed hair and gleaming white teeth. We all know that's not who they really are."

Indeed, whom do we think we're fooling? God knows. When a member of our local community—a pillar of the Catholic Church, a seemingly perfect dad with seemingly perfect children—was arrested on domestic abuse charges, someone asked me if I was surprised. In truth, I was not. I was reminded of the wisdom of my own father, who told me to be wary of anything that looks perfect on the outside. "No one, nothing, is perfect," he'd say, "and if it looks perfect that's only because someone is trying to hide something." Perhaps he was being a little cynical. Perhaps. But probably not.

Step one in any type of healing or therapy involves admitting we have a problem. Basically, it requires us to own up to our own brokenness. I'm going to admit something here that you probably shouldn't share with your children and grandchildren. It's not really a good code to live by, but, hey, I was in college. As a student, I adopted the personal mantra, "There is virtue in a certain degree of vice." This was, admittedly, a thinly veiled construct to moralize some bad decision-making. Some might even call it self-permission to sin. Maybe.

Here's where I was coming from: I had gone to a few meetings of a campus Christian organization, and while these folks were very nice and welcoming, I was taken aback by how openly critical and condemning they were of others. I saw how they viewed themselves as *saved* and everyone else as *condemned*. I would be reminded of this many years later when a Catholic filmmaker was trying to convince me to do a project with him. In our conversation, he kept referring to the world as being divided between the *sacred* and the *profane*. Finally, I asked, "Didn't God create the whole thing? The land and the water? The day and the night? How could some of it be sacred while the rest of it is profane? Is not all from God?"

He clarified that he really meant the *religious* and the *secular*. Again, I asked, "Which part is not from God?" We agreed that I wasn't a good fit for his project.

In college, I preferred the company of the *condemned* crowd. Later, I would discover that Jesus did too. These were the people I studied with, debated with, played basketball with, and broke bread with. They were open, accepting, loving, and not judgmental. I was free to be myself around them. What I learned from them is that

once you've come face-to-face with your own sinfulness—
once you've taken a drag on a joint, once you've thrown
up in an alley behind a bar, once you've (to borrow words
from Fr. Berger, my high school theology teacher) "ven-
tured below the shoulders or above the knees"—you can
no longer look down your nose at anyone else again. To be
clear, I'm not condoning any of these actions. They can be
harmful, even destructive. People get hurt. But once we
come to terms with our own brokenness and the shadow
reality that we are capable of hurting others, we open
ourselves to forgiveness, mercy, and unconditional love.
Thanks be to God!

To fully appreciate Eucharist, it is worthwhile to reflect
on the wisdom behind the penitential rite. It itches, but
think about it. What's one of the first things we do when
we come together for Mass? We all admit we're broken.
We all own up to the fact that we come as flawed pilgrims
on a journey toward wholeness, a journey we haven't yet
completed. So we basically exclaim, "I am broken, yet I
am welcomed into Christ's presence—Lord, have mercy!
I'm kind of lost and I can't really go it alone, so Jesus walks
with me—Christ, have mercy! I am learning and growing
as I journey toward wholeness, and the Holy Spirit won't
give up on me—Lord, have mercy!" We start by acknowledging that we are all, each and every one of us, a fragile
pile of pieces held together by Scotch tape and prayer.

And you know what? It's beautiful! It's the most free-
ing and liberating feeling there is! What a gift to be able
to drop all pretenses, let go of all preoccupation with
self-image, and stand honestly and vulnerably before

God, saying, "Yup, this is me. Scarred, bruised, confused, doubting, frightened, sinful. I'm not going to pretend I'm something I'm not. And yet you love me anyway?! And yet you welcome me at your table?! And yet you break yourself open and pour yourself out for me?!" Holy smokes that's powerful!

If some of the gatekeepers in the Catholic Church had been at the door of the upper room on the night of that Passover, Jesus would have dined alone. I'm not exaggerating. I realize that statement might raise some blood pressures. Well-meaning people may get defensive. Some might dismiss this entire book over it. But does it contain an element of truth?

Besides Jesus, who in that upper room was without sin? Jesus knew the score. He knew who these people were, what their salty qualities were, where they stumbled, and which edges they were rough around. He loved them anyway. He washed their feet anyway. He broke bread with them anyway. And he offered himself up for them anyway. We're no different.

We are blessed. And broken. And called to share.

Do This in Memory of Me

I n the classic Mel Brooks and Gene Wilder film *Young Frankenstein*, the new generation Igor meets the new generation Dr. Frankenstein at the train station. Igor, as you may recall, walks with a limp, and when he tells Dr. Frankenstein to "walk this way," he means it literally and hands over his cane. The perplexed doctor follows suit, hunches over the cane, and limps down the stairs. It's a classic piece of brilliant comedy. The twist, obviously, is that *walk this way* is typically a reference to direction, not to posture or gate.

As a teenager, I delighted in teasing my family with this type of humor. Whenever my mother would ask me to set the table, I'd respond with, "Sure. Where would you like me to set it?" If someone asked me to pass the milk, I'd ask if they wanted me to pass the pitcher as well. You get the picture, and you are likely thankful you didn't know me as a teen. It can get annoying, as I would discover when my own kids hit middle school. The point in all this is to underscore that language can have a broader meaning and a narrower meaning. We typically think of the narrowest meaning as being literal, but it is also shallow. It misses the depth and substance of the broader meaning. If someone invites you for a cup of coffee, you intuitively understand the coffee is incidental. The invitation is about relationship and conversation. If we invite someone to share Eucharist with us, what do we really mean by that?

In most cases, we consider the broader meaning to be the default. This is different from the mere distinction between literal and figurative speech. We all know that when someone says they're *catching a flight* or *hopping a train*, they're being figurative, not literal. In these cases, the figurative is the broader, and only real, definition. As a comparative, when someone leaves work in a hurry and says she has to take her son to the emergency room, we recognize she's being literal, yes, but more important, we understand there is a broader meaning. The story is far bigger and more significant than the narrow understanding. She is not merely running an errand. This distinction between the concrete and the conceptual, between the narrow meaning and the broader or deeper meaning, is foundational in measuring reading comprehension and baseline intelligence.

Again, if someone invites you to share Eucharist, we all know the narrow, functional meaning. What is the broader meaning?

This is critical in applying an adult understanding of Scripture. It invites us to go beyond the basic literal vs. literary paradigm. It is also central to Jesus' communication style. When Jesus tells the rich official to sell all he has and give it to the poor (Lk 18:22), we are given to understand there's a broader meaning in play—the kingdom of heaven is not a status to be achieved or a reward to be received; it is a reality to be actualized only when we cease living for self-advancement and personal glory. From his parable about mustard seeds to his teachings about the Beatitudes, Jesus' words almost always carry both a narrower and a broader or deeper meaning. We do him a great disservice when we swim only in the narrow channel and don't open ourselves to his broader and deeper seas.

A good example in a practical application is found in our marriage vows. The promise to be faithful on a narrow scope merely means sexual exclusivity. While many people struggle with this, most couples who have been married any significant length of time will tell you that's the easier part. When we broaden our understanding of the scope, we realize *being true to you* means accepting and respecting who your partner truly is as an image of God. We do not promise *to be true to the person I want you to be.* This, it seems, is where most marriages spin into trouble. In other words, the broader meaning is the driving meaning. Relational fidelity involves a whole lot more than sexual fidelity. If we follow our understanding to an even broader scope yet, we realize the *be true to you* promise includes having faith in your partner and the journey they are walking. Spouses who've walked with a partner through a chronic physical or mental illness understand this scope like no one's business.

If you're wondering why I allowed myself to digress into a discussion about marriage in a book about Eucharist, read on, my friend! The sacredness celebrated in the communion of marriage is absolutely part of a broader scope understanding of the Communion of Eucharist. I'm starting to get way too churchy here, so I need to ratchet it back before I become someone I'm not. Keep this in mind as we journey forward—Eucharist does not belong to the Church; the Church belongs to Eucharist. If this conversation waxes churchy, it is getting too narrow. Eucharist is a life-sized idea. We need to think big.

This might be a good time to step away for a minute, stare at the sky, stretch your eyes, and deeply breathe in the gift of life.

When Jesus completes the foot washing in John's gospel and says, "As I have done for you, you should also do" (Jn 13:15), is he speaking physically or directionally? Or both? Does he literally mean that we, as disciples, ought to routinely wash each other's feet? Wisely, we have interpreted this as a reference to his larger meaning—make yourself the servant of all. We would all agree that nurses, kindergarten teachers, trash collectors, social workers, firefighters, and so many others are modern-day foot washers.

When we volunteer at the food pantry, read to residents in care facilities, help a stranger jump-start his car, or bring cookies to a single mom, we are in fact washing feet.

Likewise, when Jesus offers the imperative to "do this in memory of me" (Lk 22:19), is he talking about a literal, specific action? A directional way of life? Or both? As Catholics, we readily embrace the narrower meaning—the literal, specific action. Thus, we gather around a table and ritualize the re-creation of the event. All's good.

But there is a deeper, broader, and more profound message in the imperative *do this in memory of me,* and it hinges on a spiritual pursuit of a simple question: What is the *this* we are being asked to *do?*

Oh boy. The easy and obvious answer is exactly what we do on the surface. We gather in a room, invoke the Holy Spirit to turn bread and wine into the Body and Blood of Christ, and share it with each other. But as incredible and beautiful as this can be, let's be honest: it's the easiest and narrowest adherence to the directive to *do this in memory of me.* In fact, this is so simple that we've decided even second graders can do it. As we grow in our spirituality, however, we seek a broader and deeper understanding of the mystery. What is the action—the *do this*—beyond the narrow scope? What did Jesus actually do that he is telling us to do? I submit he did, and is instructing us to do, four things:

He took the bread and wine.
He broke himself open.
He poured himself out.
He gave himself to the others.

Before you read on, give that list some air. Give it your air. Breathe each line deeply into your lungs and hold it there for three or four or five beats of your heart before exhaling. He's not merely telling us what to do for an hour on Sunday mornings; he's showing us how to live as he lives, how to love as he loves. Jesus is role-modeling for us how to live a full and meaningful life, how to live in real presence, how to be happy. This is a heart-to-heart encounter.

It's worth restating this: Jesus is role-modeling for us how to live a full and meaningful life, how to live in real presence, how to be happy.

HE TOOK BREAD AND WINE

Everything we need to live and love is set right before us. It is the substance and essence of this world, the substance and essence of life. In taking the bread and wine right off the table from which they were all eating, Jesus is illustrating an important point: the substance of the material world provides the essence for miracles. The fruits of our labors and work of our hands provide the resources God uses to make amazing things happen.

I love that Jesus is believed to have been trained in carpentry, that he was rooted in this tradition of taking wood from trees (material from this world), and crafting it into life-holding, life-sustaining objects. As I sit here writing, I'm working at a desk I crafted using the tools and teaching I received from my father. It is the fruit of my labor and the work of my human hands, but it is also a physical manifestation of the essence of his life and love. I intentionally and prayerfully channeled the energy of his life as

I measured, cut, and sanded the wood. Indeed, is not all art an expression of the artist's soul? The best chefs, artists, musicians, gardeners, quilters, and craftsmen understand this. If you've ever wrapped yourself in a quilt made by your grandmother, or made brownies using your mother's recipe, you've experienced this as well; you know what it means for the life and love of another person to be given real presence through a material object.

Jesus, more than anyone else, would have understood the trinitarian harmony between creator, creating, and created. It expresses the relational unity—the sacred oneness—between the one doing the creating, the act of creating, and the material expression of creation. Just as my desk holds the life energy of my dad and me, the materials of this world hold the life energy of the One who created them. In the same way, your material body holds the Spirit breath of the One who created you.

It's easy to lose sight of this as we increasingly live in a prefabricated, manufactured world. As we eat glazed salmon on beds of spinach while sitting in air-conditioned restaurants, when we chow down on buffalo wings and beers while watching March Madness on giant screens in sports bars, when we grab a quick bite while flying through the Popeye's drive-through, we so easily lose the connection between creator, creating, and creation.

Without even realizing it, we become disconnected from the source and stream of our own sustenance. Grabbing prepackaged, often processed, foods off supermarket shelves, wiping barcodes across optical scanners, loading bags of groceries into trunks of cars, and driving paved roads home to modern kitchens—through it all our minds whir and stir with nary a thought about the miracle of the food that makes its way to our own tables. "When drinking the water," the Chinese proverb tells us, "Remember the one who dug the well." Eucharist calls us back to this awareness and anchoring.

He took bread and wine. He said this is me. Let it be you too.

I'm not knocking modern conveniences and conveyances. Not by any means! There are few human experiences I enjoy more than a brat and a beer at a ballgame, and I have absolutely no idea how the nachos I dip into a gelatinous cheese-like goo came to be. Openly, I admit ignorance in this matter is a privileged bliss. As the saying goes, sometimes you don't want to know how the sausage is made.

What I am saying, though, is that our modern world requires we do more spiritual work. We live at a distance that requires us to look further to see deeper. The gift of connected wholeness in our lives—reunifying Creator, creating, and creation—needs awareness and contemplation to be experienced. Eucharist gives us this. At least it should.

Unfortunately, two things have happened in our modern Church to dilute and even disconnect us from the full impact of the experience. First, we've lost the the idea and experience of offertory as a sense of the offering of our lives.

For an overwhelming majority of Catholics, the term *offertory* is merely archaic churchspeak and has been replaced with *collection,* a term with no intuitive or meaningful connection to Eucharist at all. If you ask nearly any Catholic lay person why we *take up the collection* (that's the language we use) at the start of the Liturgy of the Eucharist, most will look at you with a blank stare and wonder what you mean by *Liturgy of the Eucharist.* They understand what *take up the collection* means, but the understanding of its connection with Eucharist remains superficial.

This is another example of theological reductionism. We've taken this beautiful idea of offertory, the action of offering up the work of our hands—the fruits of our labors—to be blessed, broken, and shared, and we've reduced it to a seemingly obligatory financial tax for sitting in the pew. How can we ever fully enter the profound wonder of Eucharist if we don't connect our own lives, our own work and energy, to it? When we look upon the elements on the altar, the bread and wine, do any of us truly see them as the fruits of our labors and the works of our hands? Do we see them as the elements of God's creation transformed by human labor into bread and wine, and now offered back to God to be transformed again into the substance and essence of Christ? Do we see them as the collective gifts of the gathered community being offered up, consecrated, and shared? Do we see them as the circular unity between Creator, creating, and created?

Second, we lost the authenticity of the elements.

My parents had a box-sized roulette game that came with quarter-sized poker chips. As kids, we used the white chips for communion wafers when we played church. Yes, poker chips. It never occurred to us to use bread because communion wafers don't look anything like bread. They look like small poker chips. I asked once if we could use potato chips, but my mom said no, we couldn't use junk food for communion.

I've eaten in a lot of restaurants in my lifetime. Nearly all serve bread in one form or another. Yeast breads aside, I've eaten all sorts of flat breads, pita breads, and flour tortillas over the years. None of them had the look, feel, texture, or taste of a communion wafer. People joke about communion wafers tasting like cardboard, but the truth is that the only thing resembling the taste of a communion wafer is another communion wafer. I am aware of no real food like it.

Shape, size, and taste aside, the actual disconnect has to do with the fact that these things are pressed, manufactured, and packaged by machines in factories. Not only do communion wafers fail to resemble bread by any measure, they are not really the work of human hands, nor are they the gifts of the community. What, exactly, are we offering up?

When Jesus instituted Eucharist, substance and essence mattered. The elements mattered. He did not use an approximation of bread and wine; he used the real thing, taken right from the table from which they were eating. Yes, it was a Passover meal, so the bread was unleavened. But it was familiar. It was bread.

Allow me to reel this back in. I'm not arguing with collection baskets and wafers. The collection plate represents the gifts of the community; it represents the work of human hands. But when engaged through human experience, this connection is not intuitive. We need to think broader and deeper to understand. Likewise, in most parishes, the wafers we use for communion are not actually made from bread brought forth from the kitchens of the gathered people. In fact, they do not really resemble anything we would actually serve as food when the family gathers for Thanksgiving. Again, the connection is not intuitive. We need to engage broader, deeper thinking to understand.

HE BROKE
HIMSELF OPEN

Stress does unfortunate things to our bodies. It raises our blood pressure, upsets our digestion, causes insomnia, disrupts our sex drive, increases depression, and causes us to binge watch old episodes of *The Beverly Hillbillies*. Not good. It also messes with our brains. Stress gremlins override hormone production levels and scramble our circuitry. They're like prankster high school kids in a '50s-era comedy.

Bottom line, stress and anxiety cause us to be self-focused, self-absorbed, and self-protective. Our brains respond to stress the same way they respond to illness. When we feel sick, such as when we have a bad cold or the flu, our overriding response is to cocoon. We want to isolate from everyone, wrap ourselves in a blanket, curl up in bed, and watch Netflix. Our relationships with others become primarily needs-based, and we expect them to respond to our need for peace and quiet, our need for a glass of water, our need to be left alone.

When most of us are under the weather, we naturally feel a little self-entitled. That's how we're built, and for good reason. We are hardwired to prioritize self-care at those times so we can return to health. Likewise, we are predisposed to self-isolate so as not to infect other members of our household or tribe. Thus, when we're ill, we give ourselves full permission morally and socially to live selfishly.

Increasingly, however, we seem to generalize this response to all of life's inevitable discomforts. When we're injured, when we're frustrated, when we're stuck in traffic, when we're annoyed, when the line is too long at Starbucks, when we're offended, when our egos are threatened, basically whenever the earth doesn't spin to our liking, we recoil within ourselves and focus on self-interest. Our response to all these stressors is to prioritize self-comfort. And we live with a lot of stressors.

Good high school coaches tell their players that maturity is achieved when we learn to be comfortable with discomfort. Only then will our minds stay focused even though a cold rain is falling or our legs are tired. This is an important part of teamwork. It's how we continue to serve the interests of the group while setting aside personal self-interest. Living in real presence with one's teammates, one's coworkers, or one's spouse means being fully present to the needs of the whole, even when the cost must be paid in the currency of self-sacrifice.

The life lessons in this are obvious. By the way, they're also what the image of a crucifix represents. It's what this whole faith is ultimately all about—the willingness to break oneself open bodily, mindfully, and spiritually, to accept and even embrace personal vulnerability, in order to be one with others. Perhaps most compellingly, this is what it means to love, and it is at the same time the most challenging, the most rewarding, the most human, and the most sacred of all life experiences.

Jesus' words "Do this in memory of me" present us with a much bigger task than we're often comfortable admitting. He's asking us to break ourselves open as he did, and to be vulnerable as he was. That's hard. Really hard. Pinned against the earth under the weight of stresses and anxieties, we'd rather be self-protective, self-defensive, self-interested, and self-advancing. Break ourselves open? Be vulnerable? No thank you. No wonder we're comfortable reducing Eucharist to an object rather than an action, to a wafer rather than a way of life. It may be safer to stop at merely receiving the Eucharist, but it's so much more enriching and rewarding to receive, become, and share the Eucharist.

When my friend Tony and I started StreetLights Outreach, it was as vulnerable and exposing as I had ever felt not only as a Christian but as a human being. This was as raw as faith gets. StreetLights Outreach started as a feet-on-the-street late night ministry of direct engagement and encounter. No rules, no structures, no programs, no system or organization. We were just two guys sitting on lawn chairs on a corner in an at-risk neighborhood from ten to midnight on a Friday or Saturday night.

When we asked ourselves *how Jesus did church,* the answer was rather radical and shocking. Jesus did church face-to-face on the streets, at the shore, on the hillside, in boats, and at the well. Basically, Jesus did church wherever there were people. He did not do church behind brick walls or stained-glass windows. And, yes, of course he went to the synagogue and the temple, but he didn't set up shop there. Certainly, it would have been safer to operate, teach, and preach within the structures of the religion, but Jesus didn't want to simply break open the books of the Torah, he wanted to break open himself, the very embodiment of Christ. *Do this* in memory of me.

He Poured Himself Out

I awoke one morning in my late twenties feeling overwhelmed. I had a wife, a child, a home, a mortgage, and a job. Somehow. I had never really planned any of it. From the outside looking in, I had become a grown-up. Somehow. This was the American dream, yet I didn't feel fulfilled. Or accomplished. Or even satisfied. I felt overwhelmed, anxious, and even fraudulent. My mind began racing toward the day that lay before me—the things I needed to get done, the meetings I would be attending, the expectations people would place on me. Self-doubt, questions, fear, and resentment began to bubble up. How will the day go? How will people respond to me in meetings? How will they like the work I would be presenting? Will they be impressed? Will they even like me?

Staring at the ceiling, I thought there must be a better way. There must be a better way to go through life. I took a deep breath. Then another.

Then, in a flash, I was struck by a thought—a question actually. Was I living backwards? What if, I wondered... what if instead of being so preoccupied with how the day's events would impact me, I thought instead about how I would impact them? What if instead of being anxious about whether people would find something to like and admire in me, I focused on finding something to like and admire in them? What if instead of investing my energy on thoughts about how the world would impact me today, I invested my energy on how I would impact the world?

What if instead of being self-referencing I chose to be others-referencing?

I started anticipating my day again, thinking about my schedule. But this time instead of wondering how the experiences and encounters of the day would affect my life, I thought about how the experiences and encounters of the day would be presenting opportunities for me to affect the lives of others.

Suddenly the day felt different. I felt different. There was no stress, no anxiety. I couldn't wait to spring from bed and engage. Such a simple thought, an easy exercise. Instead of focusing on how people and experiences affect me, I would reverse the flow of my energy and focus on how I affect them.

The spiritual gift of that simple clarity changed the way I saw everything. It changed the way I've thought about life from that day forward.

Most of us have a default tendency to live life from the outside-in. We're preoccupied with how the world, events, and people around us affect our sense of happiness, security, and well-being. It's a self-referential way of being, placing ourselves as the purpose and object of our daily life. We can't even imagine a different way. We then go about the business of trying to orchestrate and manipulate situations, people, and even public policy to conform accordingly, to give ourselves the most favorable experience. When we are unhappy, agitated, or uncomfortable, we automatically start looking for what or who needs to change in the world around us.

That's not how Jesus lived. His energy was outflowing, focused on how he could bring healing, growth, and comfort to others. Rather than being the master of his own life, he became the servant of others. He talked about this quite often and openly.

Do you see the difference—living outside-in versus inside-out? It's really about the directional flow of love and energy in our lives. One way starts with the assumption that my life is all about me, but the other starts with the premise that I am about it.

When Jesus heals the blind, touches the leper, calms the storm, sits with the woman at the well, dines with the tax collectors, and institutes Eucharist, what's in it for him? His entire existence is lived with an outflowing of love, compassion, and mercy. With the exception of the woman anointing his feet with oil, we have nary a story of Jesus receiving an inflow of love. This doesn't mean people didn't love Jesus; clearly, they did. But such was not the direction of flow in his life. He lived from the inside-out, and then told us to *do this* in memory of him.

Arguably, all three of the temptations he faces in the desert are voices telling him (and us) to live from the outside-in. C'mon, the voices tell him, use your gifts and talents for self-advancement. Make yourself comfortable. Make yourself powerful. Buy a house on a hill and join a country club. Protect yourself from vulnerability. Hmmm. Now would be a good time to stare into a campfire, toast a marshmallow, and ask ourselves this soul-searching question: Is this how we live? Do we live from the outside-in, mostly looking out for ourselves?

But...but...but...what about self-care? (Please forgive me while I argue with myself for a moment.) I mean, this breaking yourself open and pouring yourself out business, why, it can be depleting. Sometimes I honestly need to spend all day walking in the woods, tinkering in the workshop, or getting lost in a good book. After all, even Jesus knew when he needed to retreat to a mountain, a garden, or the other side of the lake. Certainly, we need to step aside and recharge. Surely, we can't be giving of ourselves all the time.

Indeed, the spiritually healthy person lives in unity and harmony with the Body of Christ. Few people are more annoying than those who are simultaneously ascetic and narcissistic. I know someone like that. He's drunk on ironic self-denial, always more than ready to humble-brag about how simply he lives compared to all the self-indulgent, greedy people like me who will occasionally indulge in a juicy steak and a smooth bourbon. Yeah, I get it. I'm a sinner, and often I do things simply because they bring me joy—like watching late night episodes of *Seinfeld*, even though they offer no benefit to anyone else. And for my money, eating rationed portions of wheat germ and bean sprouts would be more about self-loathing than self-denial. But that's just me.

When Jesus said *do this in memory of me*, he was enjoying a good meal surrounded by friends.

Here's the thing: whether we're driven by self-advancement or self-denial, we're still living a life that's focused on the self. In either case, my life is all about me. And as discussed earlier, we are so programmed to live outside-in, focused on how my relationships (with creation, society, God, others, and even self) affect me, that we struggle to even imagine living a life that flows in the other direction.

Now comes the hard part, the honest come-to-Jesus moment when we stand before the mirror and look into our naked hearts. In our individualistic way of life—our ego-driven way of thinking—we are so fixated on the inward self-serving flow of experience that, if we're not careful, we even apply this directional flow to our faith and our spirituality. And why wouldn't we? We apply it to every other dimension of our lives—our birthdays, our jobs, even our marriages. If I hear one more bride refer to her wedding as *my special day,* I'll consider moving a candle too close to her veil. I always say a prayer for the groom when I hear that. That's not a celebration of love, union, and the bond of marriage; that's a celebration of *me!* Perhaps I'm being a little uncharitable. After all, we are each created in God's image and likeness, and that's worth celebrating. But God's image is an outflow of creative, unconditional love, so we might ask ourselves if that's the image of God we project into the world.

On a recent Sunday morning, I welcomed a visitor into our church's gathering space. As I walked with him, I learned he was visiting from South Carolina and was in town to meet the parents of his daughter's fiancé. He found our January weather to be surprising, but he thanked me for the warmth of the church. He then asked me to direct him to "the cry room."

I gestured toward a spacious side chapel where parents often retreat with restless children, while offering, "There's plenty of room for you to join us in the main church."

He politely shook his head, saying. "I'll be fine in here. I just came to get my Eucharist. I have no need to be around any of these other people."

This is delicate. As an introvert myself, the father of a son with highly functional Asperger's, and having familiarity with social anxieties, I wholeheartedly appreciate the various dispositions people bring. It's so important that we meet people where they're at and support them as they authentically pilgrim forward into the mysteries of life.

That being said, the Body and Blood of Christ is a reality that flows through us and animates us; it is not merely something we receive. It is an experience in which we participate, not an object we possess. To think otherwise is theological reductionism. When we show up at church to *get my Eucharist*, we essentially objectify Christ. Think about that. We reduce the Body of Christ to an object we consume for our benefit. Given the totality of everything Jesus taught and the example he set with his life, it is hard to imagine this is all he meant when he said *do this in memory of me.*

HE GAVE HIMSELF TO OTHERS

S imon Sinek, a modern business culture guru, preaches the doctrine of WHY. The golden secret of success, he professes, is to start with and stay focused on your WHY. It's a helpful insight for most of life. Motivation matters. Motivation drives attitude, and attitude drives and sustains action. Most of us get so spun up in the WHATs of life, the tasks of the day, that we lose sight of why we're doing any of it in the first place. Each time this happens, we unwittingly disconnect from our motivation; we lose the joy of our relationships and actions. Activities that once brought us life start to feel heavy and drain life from us. They are reduced to things we have to do, obligations we have to meet. Often, we grow cynical and even resentful.

Research into the psychology of motivation bears this out. When motivation becomes external (obligation, paycheck), the corresponding activity is engaged as *work*, but when the motivation is internal (our personal WHY), the same activity is engaged with gusto. Through the example of his life, Jesus shows and tells us again and again to live with inner motivation (love) and an outward flow channeling that love toward God, neighbor, self, and even our enemies. As an aside, apply this to Mass attendance. By making Mass obligatory with a threat of sin, we have made the motivation external. Thus, people resist. Such is human nature. Jesus frequently confronted the tension between the law (external) and love (internal), and each time he reminds us to make love the priority. By participating in Eucharist, we internalize the very real love of Christ so we have it within us to flow outwardly into the world. The WHY for all of this ought not be obligation, sin, fear of hell, or any other external motivator; it ought to be heartfelt love.

Couples caught in the spinning tempests of family life will sometimes report that their relationship has been diluted to the lowly status of a task to manage. In the whirl of homework, youth sports, dance and piano lessons, meal planning, grocery shopping, housework, yardwork, church committees, and full-time jobs, little time and energy remains to focus on relationship. Meaningful conversation and intimacy are just more boxes to check far down on the to-do list. It's difficult to share real presence in this context. It's so important to step back from all the WHATs and go deep by refocusing on the WHY.

I've certainly seen it in myself. At StreetLights Outreach, we host block parties in marginalized neighborhoods throughout the summer. The purpose—the WHY—of these events is to build connection and community while feeding the hungry. They're very effective, indeed eucharistic, occasions, which bring a sense of normalization, belonging, stability, and security to people and neighborhoods who have struggled. Over time, they help contribute to lower anxiety and reduced crime rates. But they're also a lot of work. It takes a significant effort to plan, prepare, and grill and serve hamburgers and hot dogs for anywhere from fifty to four hundred people. Here's the most embarrassing part—I really don't do much of the work anymore. Thankfully, Tony manages the food procurement and all the logistics. Randy coordinates local musicians to provide live music at each event. Sue brings a trunk full of children's books to give away. An army of volunteers comes out to help prepare and serve. Mostly these days, I just show up to help with the set-up before and the tear-down afterward, and I spend the time in between mingling and socializing with guests and volunteers. I do less than anyone, and yet in the midst of deadlines, commitments, and a packed schedule, I sometimes see "StreetLights Outreach Block Party" on my calendar and regard it as just one more thing I have to do. On particularly busy weeks, there is a shallow part of me that secretly hopes for a rainout.

At these times, I find it emotionally and spiritually beneficial to take a step back and reconnect with the WHY. Why are these block parties valuable? Why did Tony and I originally conceive of and activate the idea? Once I refocus on the WHY, my entire attitude and disposition shifts positively. I no longer see the block parties as something that takes time and energy from my life but as joyful occasions that I am blessed to bring life to.

Here's a little pro tip: re-examine your WHY from time to time. A WHY that is self-rewarding won't be nearly as enriching, fulfilling, and motivating as a WHY that is relationship-focused. This has everything to do with the direction in which your life is flowing. Doctors who went to medical school to gain social status and earn high incomes are generally less fulfilled and happy in their careers than those who chose the profession to serve and support the health and well-being of others. Once you factor for practice culture, their overall job satisfaction tends to be lower and they are prone to burn out faster. Likewise with teachers, police officers, attorneys, accountants, and clergy. Yes, there are certainly members of the clergy across all religions who pursued the vocation for adulation, attention, approval, escapism, moral superiority, or some other self-serving interest. They're usually not fun or even comfortable to be around.

Keep in mind that this also applies to our spirituality. When asked to name the greatest commandment, Jesus did not say, "Follow all the rules so you can go to heaven." Instead, he told us to love God with all our hearts, mind, and strength, and to love our neighbors as we love ourselves. That's very relational—God, neighbor, you. It's also very eucharistic—one Body of Christ, blessed, broken, and shared. When our life's WHY pursues the mystery of this shared love, we are eternally happy people.

There is a loaves and fishes dynamic at work here. It's beautiful. As long as we're living with an inside-out flow of love, we never run out. As long as we're sharing our own God-image giftedness with others, breaking it open and pouring it out, in whatever way we are uniquely called to do so, we keep receiving more and more to pass around. If you're not careful, you might see a miracle in all this.

About five hundred years before Christ, the Greek philosopher Aristotle observed that all people want the same thing—happiness. Everything else we think we want in life (money, status, security, power, comfort, popularity, pizza, new bowling shoes) is falsely perceived to be a means that will bring us happiness. Jesus then came along and said, "malarkey." Well, he didn't really say "malarkey." He said whatever the Aramaic equivalent would have been. Either way, his point was that most of the happiness we chase is fool's gold compared to real joy. It's merely momentary, temporary happiness. Then he offered a better plan, a plan for permanent, eternal happiness: "Love one another. As I have loved you, so you also should love one another" (Jn 13:34). He says this shortly after washing the disciples' feet, at the conclusion of which he says, "I have given you a model to follow. So that as I have done for you, you should also do" (Jn 13:15). It all sounds a lot like *do this in memory of me*, wouldn't you say? Regardless of your faith, you gotta hand it to Jesus—the guy was consistent.

So far, there have been three times in my life when I was white-knuckle terrified. Four if you count the brain surgery, but that was a primal fear, which is very different from an existential fear. The three times I was gourd-numbing scared with only faith and prayer to lean into were when I got married, when I became a father, and when I was ordained. In retrospect, I suppose it sounds a bit shallow. Who would be afraid of such abundance? But in all three cases, I was committing to a life of outward flow, a life of service. I was signing up for vulnerability, and I was afraid of losing myself.

Holy smokes, that's the big piece right there—fear of losing oneself. That'll freeze us in our tracks. In becoming a spouse, a parent, a minister, I was afraid of losing my own self-identity right at a time when my life was becoming interesting. Moreover, I was afraid of losing control of my own freedom and decision-making. Eek! There would be obligations and expectations. I would be responsible to and for other people. Frankly, I wasn't even crazy about taking responsibility for myself.

Giving over our lives to and for others is different from giving up our lives. It's the difference between commitment and surrender. When we commit to marriage and family, we're not surrendering. We're not losing ourselves. In fact, it is in this giving that we receive. We become part of and contribute to something so much bigger than we could ever be individually. We become part of and contribute to the body of Christ.

Offer yourself up, the teacher says. Break yourself open and pour yourself out. Keep your heart centered on the WHY—loving relationship with Creator and creation—and share yourself generously and lovingly with those relationships. This is the way to eternal joy. *Do this* in memory of me.

Part Three

Real Presence.
Real
Relationships.

Thanksgiving where I grew up was so cliché it's almost unreal. It was one small town prodigal daughter away from being a Hallmark Christmas movie. Lots of immediate and extended family gathered around a huge table, telling stories, sharing laughter, passing endless platters and bowls heaped with stuffing, turkey, potatoes, cranberries—you get the picture. We were of differing ilks—young/old, male/female, urban/rural, conservative/liberal, wealthy/poor, and so forth. Around this table, though, we were one—one family, one love, one body of Christ. Our differences didn't make us separate, they made us whole.

The Thanksgiving dinner during my freshman year of college took a turn when I brought up gender discrimination in corporate America. For context, I was eighteen, idealistic, and entirely ignorant about corporate America. But because I was eighteen, idealistic, and entirely ignorant, I was confident I knew what was wrong with everyone else. "It's the system," I proclaimed as if I was having an original thought. "Gender bias is institutional. There are glass ceilings everywhere. Women get paid only seventy percent of what men get paid for the same job. And they get promoted at a far lower rate." I tried to say it with a faux sophistication while holding my wine glass in a way that punctuated my points before raising it to my lips as a definitive period to settle the matter.

"Hmmm, none of that is true," my uncle Bert responded. I had expected admiration, not disagreement. I had expected to be affirmed, not contradicted. Now I would have to defend my statements against a very worthy opponent. Uncle Bert lived and breathed the corporate life. He was an executive at a large pharmaceutical company, well-traveled, well-read, and well-educated. "The threat of discrimination lawsuits is far too real," he explained. "Corporations have been forced to change. They have policies and protocols in place to make sure that doesn't happen."

"Policies can be a sugarcoat," I said. I knew I was getting in over my head, but that didn't stop me. I wasn't going to back down and risk losing face. "Corporations hide behind policy statements that don't necessarily reflect what's happening in the trenches. At ground level, individual managers find their own rationale to perpetuate discrimination." I was surprised to see Uncle Bert raise an eyebrow, subtly acknowledging that my return volley had indeed brought more insight than my original serve.

Back and forth we went, all the way through the pumpkin and mincemeat pies. We talked about the differences between the orchestrated cultures of large corporations and the looser cultures of small and mid-sized businesses where most people work. We spoke of the legacy gap and what to do about it, acknowledging that even as companies make strides, women were underrepresented in C-suites and on corporate boards. We even debated gender bias in government and religion. But here's what I remember most fondly about that conversation: at no point did either of us go off topic or make it personal. Uncle Bert never accused me of being young, ignorant, over my head, or full of myself, even though I was. He let me be me, a young man growing and discovering his own intellect and values. And at no point did I accuse him of being a self-satisfied, establishment, out-of-touch, wealthy white male. I sincerely respected him. Instead, we grew closer. Our differences brought us into unity with each other.

As the last sips of coffee were drained from the cups, Uncle Bert pushed his chair back, looked at me, and said, "If you're so concerned about gender equality, then I think you and I should do all these dishes while the women go sit down and relax." A loud cheer and laughter broke out. I grabbed some plates and headed for the kitchen where he and I continued our conversation as I washed and he dried the dishes.

What happened here? Was this Thanksgiving a eucharistic encounter? Was it sacramental? Was it, in fact, church? To understand and appreciate what happens on the altar during Mass, we need to first understand what happened around that Thanksgiving table at my parents' house. We simply cannot go to the depth of mystery if we don't first go to the depth of our own experiences. Life is like that. Wisdom comes from experience, and God is revealed to us through those experiences. If in our busyness and superficial preoccupations we water-bug our way across the surface of life, we kind of miss the point. We learn nothing. But if we pause, take a deep breath, and prayerfully contemplate our encounters along this pilgrimage called life, why it's amazing how bountifully the Holy Spirit will consecrate our lives!

But first we need to affirm that Eucharist is not merely an object or a ritual. It's a reality. It's the shared encounter with—and an experience of—the real presence of Christ in flesh and blood. We engage it poignantly at Mass, and we share it experientially in life. Hopefully, we're generous with both. Without this braided harmony of spiritual and experiential, life is cardboard, and we are merely paper dolls struggling to find depth while feeling terrified of water.

The gospels provide all sorts of parallel stories as a frame of reference for us to understand and relate. Jesus breaks bread and shares himself with Pharisees, with fishermen, with Martha and Mary, with Zacchaeus the tax collector, with prostitutes, and with his disciples. The diversity is brilliant. Rich and poor, male and female, saint and sinner—Jesus uses the occasion of breaking bread to bring people of all stripes into his very real presence. He seeks communion with them before ever asking them to amend their ways, and he never diminishes them or puts them down personally. Instead, he affirms their dignity and loves them as they are. All of them. And in the end, he looks at us and says *do this* in memory of me.

That's exactly what happened around that Thanksgiving table. It's also what should be happening at Mass. For communion to happen, there must first be an openness to entering healthy, honest relationships and dialog with people who share perspectives different from our own.

Specifically, Eucharist calls us into and shows us how to unite in five different types of relationships: with God, with self, with others, with society, and with creation. This is how we live in wholeness and harmony. If any of these relationships is false—if we don't bring our authentic self, our real presence to them—we will live with disconnect, disunity, and disharmony. Look around. Do you see any disunity or disharmony in our world? Yeah. It's everywhere, even in the Church. Why? Because we're living out of communion with God, with self, with each other, and with all of creation.

The thing about these relationships is that they're progressive. They ripple outward. If you are not in an authentic relationship of real presence with your Creator, how can you possibly live in real presence with the authentic self who was created in God's image and likeness? It simply cannot happen. And if you are not in a relationship of real presence with self, you cannot bring real presence into relationship with others. Do you see how this either builds upon itself or snowballs into turmoil?

REAL PRESENCE IN OUR RELATIONSHIP WITH GOD

My father always drove Fords. Honestly, I don't know why, but he loved cars and he always chose Fords. I think it had something to do with 1957 and a black Ford Fairlane. I'm sure there are stories he never shared with me. Some of my earliest memories involved hopping into the car with him on Saturday mornings for a trip to the lumber yard to procure whatever materials were needed for that weekend's project. These were happy, stress-free trips. As I grew into my preteen years, a friction emerged between my dad and me. It became increasingly clear we had different interests. Somehow, though, when we jumped into the Ford, we found common ground. Differences disappeared, making room for love between father and son. We even bridged our different tastes in music. Arguably, the 1971 Ford Mercury Monterey became a cathedral of its own merit. I drive Fords to this day, and I'm really not interested in looking at anything else. It's completely irrational. I don't care. Most of the best things in life bring us beyond rational. Thank God for that!

Marketing psychologists call this a brand imprint. It refers to the initial thoughts and emotions connected with our very first impressions of a brand or product. For me, I connected one particular brand of automobile with joy, comfort, love, and togetherness. It wasn't about the car at all; it was about relationship.

What's your brand imprint of God?

A few years ago, I pulled my Ford F-150 in for an oil change in Denver, Colorado. I was on my way into the mountains for a few days of backpacking, and I wanted the oil changed before heading to higher altitudes. The shop's proprietor suddenly came running up to me with great urgency. He had noticed my Green Bay Packers license plates, and he was filled with questions and stories. Was I from Green Bay? Yes. Did I ever go to games? Yes. Had I ever been inside the team's facilities? Yes. This man, whom I had never met, went on to tell me about watching Packers games as a child with his dad and his grandpa. He talked about how these were the happiest times in his life, and how he now watches all the Packers games with his own son. He opened himself to me and shared his story. We bonded. His brand imprint of the Green Bay Packers was unshakable. It wasn't about football at all; it was about relationship. And my brand imprint of him and his auto service shop was all about joy, good memories, and friendliness. It had nothing to do with an oil change; it was about relationship.

I ask again, what's your brand imprint of God? What's your brand imprint of Eucharist? Don't rush for an answer. Give yourself time to walk with the question, to remember the first images and experiences you were given, and to contemplate how they affect your emotions to this day.

Most of us were first introduced to God at a very young age by parents who, while loving, didn't really understand God themselves. In fairness, do any of us really? Nonetheless, our imprint of God was initially and understandably simple. It was primarily affected by our relationship with our dominant parent. Some of us were thus introduced to a God who is loving, comforting, benevolent, and merciful. Others, however, were introduced to a God who is both rewarding and punishing, encouraging and threatening, consoling and wrathful. And sadly, some of us were introduced to a God who is manipulative, controlling, unpredictable, and even violent. In all cases, we extended human attributes to God. After all, that was our frame of reference, and we really didn't know or understand anything else. God became a "Super Being" whom we personified according to the relationship imprint we first formed.

Although we were introduced to grander constructs over the years—God is the great I AM; God is the alpha and the omega; God is the life energy of all creation; God is love—few of us were blessed with teachers who guided us into deep mystery, so we clung to what we knew, what was comfortable. Eventually, our image of God either remained relatively juvenile, became distant and unrelatable, or became increasingly undefinable. Three distinct paths emerged: 1) continue to see God as a "Guy in the Sky" who functions as a grand puppet master for better or worse, or 2) stop believing in God altogether because the inherited image is too superficial for believability, or 3) spend our lives searching for solid footing apart from these extremes. Most adults have grown beyond our juvenile images of God, but we haven't grown beyond belief in God nor do we want to. If anything, we seek a deeper belief. Our adult spirituality churns an abiding hunger for insight into the profound mystery of life and love.

Eucharist gives us that rock-solid footing. But we have to look deep.

To understand that Eucharist is not simply some sort of Jesus pill, it helps to first expand our understanding of *God*, and second to re-examine our relationship with this infinite life-giving oneness in love we call God.

Let me pump the breaks for a minute and roll onto the shoulder. It sounds audacious, doesn't it? Expand our understanding of God? Whom are we kidding? I can't even understand the popularity of TikTok—it seems pointless. Albert Einstein reportedly said he wanted only to know the mind of God. When I first learned this, I thought that would be a worthwhile life pursuit. Later, as age introduced me to more wisdom, I realized Einstein was joking. He was being facetious. Even he, one of the most brilliant minds in human history, recognized that God is unknowable.

But if life and death teach us anything, it's that unknowable does not mean unbelievable.

The most divine things in life are not meant to be known; they can only be experienced. Sunrises and sunsets, the feeling while standing on top of a mountain, a beer with a friend, falling in love, forgiveness, bare feet in a saltwater surf, the way music stirs the soul, ice cream on a Sunday afternoon, the giggle of a toddler—these things and so much more, in fact everything good in life, are not really meant to be known or even understood. They are meant to be experienced. Such is the gift of our humanity, the sacred gift of life itself. Such is the very real presence of Christ in our lives and the heart of mystery in Eucharist: like love, it is not meant to be known or understood; it is meant to be encountered, entered, and experienced.

We never grow deeper or love more by knowing more. We do so by virtue of our heartfelt, soul-stirring experiences and relationships. This is something the saints and mystics understand intuitively that the rest of us keep struggling to figure out. We can't learn to swim by thinking about it, reading about it, or even praying about it. At some point, we have to jump in the water, splash feverishly, and find ourselves in over our heads. That's just how life works. It's also how love works. And it's exactly what Jesus did.

As Christ, the very incarnation of God's own self, plunged completely into the full experience of life, so must we as beings created in God's own image. At some point, we learn to recognize that rolling up our sleeves and plunging both arms into the clay of life, just as God did in our creation story, is a very sacred endeavor. We are not here as consumers of life but as co-creators of life, called to break ourselves open, pour ourselves out, and share ourselves abundantly. Indeed, it really is better to give than to receive. *Do this* in memory of me.

A life of love is not a spectator sport. It is an experience, an encounter, here and now. Many of us have had a heavenly, quasi-theoretical relationship with God since early childhood, and we talk about meeting God face-to-face in the afterlife. But would we even recognize this God? In truth, rather than loving God, we mostly love our notion of God, our imprint of God. This is very difficult to self-admit, but I encourage you to let down your defenses and examine your own imprint of God. Many of us are worshiping an idea while keeping ourselves at a safe distance from the reality—like a child clinging to the side of the pool. That's one of the conveniences of a heaven that places God's kingdom *out there* and *up there* in the afterlife rather than right here right now. By imaging God in the beyond, I don't have to deal with God in the homeless person on the corner or the annoying coworker who heats fish in the microwave.

The projection of an image, however, is a poor substitute for an experience. Eucharist brings us into the real presence of an earthly (fruit of the vine and work of human hands) relationship with God. We become one with Christ and, in that, one with God. This isn't new; we've all been taught it. We know it. But it continues to be a lot of gobbledygook church-speak. We say it. We profess to believe it. But we don't experience it. What's going on?

Upon participating in Holy Communion at Mass, I returned to my pew and knelt like everyone else. This time I looked around and wondered why. I'm told to kneel out of reverence for the Eucharist, but I've also been told that by this point in the Mass we have become Eucharist. We have become the living body and blood of Christ. We have encountered, we have experienced, we have engaged, and we have become one with God. One in the Spirit. One in the Lord. And so have all the others around us. That's the whole point! So why are we still kneeling? Why aren't we on our feet, singing in joy, ready to run into the world and do the work of Christ? Perhaps we need to kneel just to take in the significance of it all—like an Olympian who drops to her knees after winning the gold medal.

As I contemplated all this, I noticed how everyone remained kneeling until the sacrament was returned to the tabernacle. Then we sat down. I recalled how Sr. Mary Alice taught us in the second grade to remain kneeling out of respect until "Jesus is put away." What sort of mind-numbing nonsense is this? Are the leftover hosts somehow more Body of Christ than the people who have just participated in this Holy Communion? Not if we really believe what we profess! Granted, we kneel out of reverence for Christ's very real presence in the Eucharist, but does our practice inadvertently maintain a distance between us, our neighbors, and the very real presence of Christ we have all become part of? The whole point of Eucharist, indeed the whole point of Jesus' entire life, is to erase that distance.

Eucharist—as a profound experience to be engaged and shared, not merely as an object to be received—unites us in a deeper relationship with God. We become the body of Christ. And to be clear, that's not a metaphor. We share in and become the very real presence of Christ in the world. Honestly, that should get us off our knees and on our feet. The Body and Blood of Christ should get our own bodies moving and our own blood pumping. But we have to be willing to plunge into it, all of it, holding nothing back. Ahh, there's the rub.

REAL PRESENCE IN OUR RELATIONSHIP WITH SELF

The challenge with really getting to know oneself is that the deeper we go, the more the landscape keeps changing. Our pilgrimage through life becomes like a trek through the mountains. There are arduous climbs, treacherous descents, and extended periods of plateaus. And when we finally arrive at a summit and gain perspective on who we are, we look up and see another mountain range ahead, and another after that. The horizon keeps moving. The deeper we go, the more we discover we are as unknowable as God. This is the beginning of a true spiritual awakening. My authentic identity, the real presence of who I am, is not a being apart from creation, but being one with creation.

That's a lot. And it makes our egos uneasy. We like being the star of our own show, the hero in the dramatic comedy of our own life. We want to be special and stand out, stand apart, and even stand above. So rather than trek through those metaphorical hills and valleys of self-discovery only leading to self-surrender, it's so much easier to fly over the range, keeping both life and faith relatively superficial. Why go to the gym and work out when I can sit in my chair and criticize athletes on television? Why go to a therapist and unpack my trauma when I can stir the ice in my drink while smugly criticizing everyone else? Why go to the shelter and wash the feet of the homeless when I can log on to social media and blame an opposing political party for all the suffering in the world?

I tried to teach all three of my sons as they were growing that character is revealed in adversity. It's relatively easy for any of us to be the best version of ourselves when the sun is shining, the breeze is at our back, and we get the big promotion. But who are we when the inevitable storms of life hit, when the game is lost, when the biopsy comes back positive? Who are we when our dreams are shattered, all seems lost, and the endless night descends upon broken relationships?

It's so much easier, isn't it, to simply sit in the car and cruise through life with the radio on, viewing the scenery through the windows? Why get out, lace up our boots, and hike through the mountains where we encounter our own weakness, fragility, and vulnerability? Welcome to the metaverse—and thank you, Mark Zuckerberg and Silicon Valley, for making it possible to coast through a virtual reality where we never have to confront the humiliations of God's actual reality. Artificial presence is so much easier and far less risky than real presence, and we get to be the star of our own show.

Sadly, this virtual reality business is not new. It's merely the most modern manifestation of an age-old concept. For millennia, humans have been trying to orchestrate and manipulate reality to better fit personal self-interest. This is what the leaders in the Roman Empire were trying to do. It's what the Temple authorities were trying to do. And it's what Jesus was trying to open everyone's eyes to recognize.

Even today, people use political structures and social policy to advance personal self-interest with little regard for the impact on others. We are tempted and even encouraged to look the other way while people suffer, as long as we don't have to suffer ourselves. We even use religion to step back and escape the ardors of reality rather than using it as a framework with which to approach reality. Admittedly, I'm being a little harsh here. Perhaps even unfair. We all need to step away from time to time. But the larger point remains—the deep life that opens us to growth and discovery is not accessible from the comforts on the surface. It requires a commitment of real flesh and blood.

We have been taught there are two options when faced with adversity: fight and flight. Do we dig in and fight? Or do we run and hide? The problem with these two options is that both are fueled by self-preservation. When the going gets tough, we typically retreat into self-interest, even when our objectives are noble.

Jesus, in his moment of truth, introduces us to a third option: to love. Certainly, he was tempted to fight—

indeed, someone brought swords along to the garden on that night. And certainly, he would have been tempted to flee—run away and live to serve another day. But Jesus' thinking was never self-indulgent or self-directed. In the moment of greatest adversity, he chooses to give of his own flesh and blood so that love—not hatred or fear but love—would rule the day.

During the height of the pandemic, when health-care workers were overwhelmed and understaffed, I had an opportunity to interview several doctors and nurses who had been working on the front lines. These people were physically fatigued, emotionally exasperated, and spiritually exhausted. We talked about the deaths they witnessed, the hands they held, the families they had journeyed with, and I asked each of them if there was anything they'd like to say to the community. Many of them looked back at me and said, "I want people to know we will care for them. I want them to know that no matter what they think or believe about Covid, no matter what their political stance has been on masks or vaccines, when they or someone in their family gets sick with this virus, they can come here, and we will give them all the compassionate care they need."

I was so impressed. These doctors and nurses had been traversing the endless mountains of stark reality. They held suffering in their own hands and hearts. And they had discovered a deeper truth about themselves—they were not going to dive into the political fight, nor were they going to run away from it. Instead, they were going to keep giving of themselves, loving neighbors, even loving enemies, washing feet, breaking themselves open, pouring themselves out.

What I have done for you, you should do for one another, Jesus said.

Character, Jesus shows us in Eucharist, is revealed in adversity. And the person of Christlike character does not fight or flee. Those of Christlike character choose a third option, a better option—to give their own lives over to love. Do this in memory of me.

REAL PRESENCE IN OUR RELATIONSHIPS WITH OTHERS

The man's eyes welled with tears. He hadn't even told me his name yet, but he was opening his life's wounds and letting me put my hand gently inside. Tony and I had been standing on the corner for nearly two hours when this guy and another man rolled up in a car and asked what we were doing. I gave him the normal StreetLights Outreach spiel, explaining that we were just out there to be present, give folks someone to talk to, maybe help them find a meal or a shelter if needed. I expected them to drive on.

Instead, he jumped out of the car and walked over to me with his hand extended. I took it—held it actually—and noticed his eyes were already filled with tears. He explained how he had been homeless a year earlier and how lost and lonely he had felt. He shared his story and opened his vulnerability to me, and in doing so let me reach in and touch the Christ in him.

How many times have I been so blessed! How many times have others through life and death extended to

101

me the same generous love Jesus extended to Thomas? Normally, we try to disguise our wounds and hide our vulnerability. We don't want others to see how broken we really are. But when we open ourselves to each other in that way, Christ lives! We become believers.

I have to ask myself if I've allowed others to see and touch my wounds. Have I been too proud? Too shy? Too aloof? Too self-protective?

When we hear the story of doubting Thomas, we tend to identify with the skeptical apostle. We understand him. We relate. On some level, however, we're also a bit embarrassed for him. Yet he was the only one who asked Jesus if he could touch his vulnerability, his brokenness, his humanness. And Jesus let him! Jesus opened not just his hands and his side, but also his heart, his soul, and the essence of who he is.

In our current world, the phrase "I feel ya" is a slang expression for "I understand and empathize with you." It's an expression of relationship, care, and intimacy. You hurt and I feel ya. In asking to touch Jesus' wounds, Thomas is asking, "Can I feel ya? Will you open yourself up to me? Will you allow me to empathize with you and understand you? Will you let me touch you and love you in your vulnerability?" Jesus, of course, says yes.

I learned on the streets that I have no right to judge another person. I don't know what floggings, thorns, and crosses they've borne. I don't know what price they've paid for the sins of others, what traumas they've had imposed upon them. But when they've allowed me to touch their wounds, I've been blessed to reach into their brokenness.

This is where the risen Christ lives!

Eucharist brings us to this sacred and holy place where we dare to live beyond ego, beyond fear, beyond vanity, beyond death. It's where we dare to let others see and touch our brokenness and we love them in theirs. To receive Eucharist takes time. To participate in Eucharist takes openness. But to become Eucharist—to see Christ in others and to be Christ to others—well, that takes courage.

A life of Eucharist—through which we willingly offer the gift of self, break ourselves open, pour ourselves out, and share ourselves with one another—brings an experience of real presence to our relationships. Is this not what we experience in marriage? Parenthood? Meaningful friendships?

As I watched my mother care for my dad while his aggressive parkinsonism progressed, I was acutely aware we were witnessing the living body of Christ at work in our midst. No question this was a eucharistic relationship. In every way imaginable, this couple who had been married for fifty-seven years lived the example of real presence. It was as real and authentic as life gets. My mother lovingly gave the fruit of her labors and the work of her hands to his care. She washed his feet literally, metaphorically, and spiritually, breaking herself open and pouring herself out for him day after day. She shared her body and blood with him, and he with her. The exchange was mutual and relational. My dad, with his body so very broken, poured himself out for her in any and every way he could. When he could no longer control his facial muscles, he smiled and offered loving gratitude with his eyes. We all saw it and felt it. In the hospital toward the end, as my mom stood by his bed, he somehow managed to reach an arm out, hook her waist, and draw her close, whispering, "I love you."

Anyone who wants to argue that this is not the sacred, consecrated body of Christ alive in our midst is living a spirituality that's only ankle deep. As anyone who has walked such a journey will attest, this is a very holy communion, the very real presence of the body and blood of Christ. From second grade on, our conversations about Eucharist often focus on process and technicalities such as the structures of language, the positioning of the corporal on the altar, the posture of the presider's hands, and other practice instructions, but at the end of the day are we just looking at our watches while missing the sunrise?

This reality that Eucharist is the basis for meaningful relationships with other people may be obvious when caring for someone who is dying of a terrible disease, but it is no less present and authentic in the ordinary every day. Boiled down to its simplest terms, Eucharist makes the ordinary extraordinary. Jesus takes very ordinary bread and wine, breaks it open and pours it out, and transforms it into the Body and Blood, the substance and essence, the nourishment and vitality of the living Christ! What could possibly be more extraordinary than that? And then he tells us that we should get together and do the same—take the ordinary and make it extraordinary, take the fruits of your labors and make them holy, take the work of your hands and make it sacred—and share it with each other.

Isn't this really what love does? I happened to be quite ill with Covid-19 on my birthday, so my friend Scott set an ice cream cake and a six pack of beer on my front stoop, rang the bell, and drove away. He took two very ordinary things (cake and beer) and shared them in a way that made my life extraordinary on that day. Scott doesn't live anywhere near me, so it was a considerable trip out of his way. I was very touched and moved by the effort. This might not be Eucharist with the big E, but it is certainly eucharist with a little e, and dare I ask what the real value of Eucharist (with the big E) might be if we don't go around sharing eucharist (with the little e) on a daily basis? *Do this* in memory of me!

No, I am NOT suggesting that ice cream cake and beer left on my doorstep are equivalent to the bread and wine consecrated on the altar. But I am suggesting that in living out loving relationships with one another, Eucharist begets eucharist. What we celebrate as sacrament we live sacramentally. That's a lot of fancy-pants churchspeak, and I should apologize, but it succinctly expresses a profound truth: Christ does not live apart from us in a far-off kingdom of heaven; Christ lives within us and works through us *on earth as it is in heaven.* When we engage with a deep awareness, we begin to recognize the extraordinary in the ordinary, and we start to see all of life and all relationships as sacred. This is what it means to peel back the surface and enter a deeper spirituality. Like the incarnate Christ himself, we unify God and humanity, heaven and earth, saints and sinners. Eucharist is powerful that way.

What Scott did for me, people do for each other on a routine basis. There are two big differences, however. First, most of us do them occasionally or episodically. The saints among us (like Scott) do them as a way of life. It's almost an automatic routine for them. Scott will undoubtedly argue this is an extreme overstatement. It is not. The practice of living with a flow of love-sharing energy that moves from the inside outward is second nature to people who live deeply. It's as though they get up each day and automatically start looking for ways to wash a few feet and lift others up.

Second, while most of us reach out this way toward people we love (those with whom we are already in close relationship), the saints among us readily act this way toward complete strangers. They're living example of the good Samaritan. I know a guy who, immediately upon shoveling out his driveway after a heavy snowstorm, quickly ran out and bought a snowblower so he could clean an elderly neighbor's driveway before he came out and tried to do it himself. "I don't really know the guy," he told me. "But I always see him out there with a shovel, digging his way out. We had fourteen inches of heavy, wet snow, and I was sincerely worried about his heart and back. And I knew if I started shoveling him out, he'd immediately come outside and try to help. So I just did what any decent person who could afford it would do." He then continued to blow the snow out of his neighbor's driveway for the next twelve years. And here's the best part—he still shoveled his own driveway by hand because he wanted the exercise. He seriously bought a snowblower just to take care of an aging neighbor a few houses down the block, a guy he barely knew. Why? *I just did what any decent person would do. Do this* in memory of me.

Eucharist is given a real presence each time we love one another with no expectation of return. Do we see it? This is how Christ lived, and it's how the Body and Blood of Christ continues to live through us.

REAL PRESENCE IN OUR RELATIONSHIP WITH SOCIETY

Michelle used to cry when she dropped the kids off on the first day of school each autumn. I did not. I celebrated. I did tear up, however, at the science fair, especially the year I listened to Adam explain his process for determining how many volts of electricity it takes to make a light bulb explode. That was a proud moment! In our house, preparation for science fairs was pure madness. It typically involved keeping a fire extinguisher within arm's reach.

I also got a lump in my throat when Alex starred as Bilbo Baggins in a middle school play and when Jacob scored his first soccer goal. At a Holy Thursday Mass, tears physically ran down my face as I watched my three sons wash their mother's feet. Even the memory makes me misty.

Why does this happen? Why do we get emotional about experiences that are not even our own? Psychologists and neuroscientists will talk about empathy and its role in society, but parents know there is something more, something deeper, going on. When we watch our children grow, discover, and emerge into the fullness of the images of God they were each created to be—even as they stumble, falter, and inevitably fail along the way—we become acutely aware that they are we and we are they. We must keep this to ourselves, holding it in our hearts, because they will break into cold sweats and convulsions if we speak it out loud. Seriously. Try telling your fifteen-year-old daughter that you and she are really just different versions of the same person. Drop me a note and let me know how it goes. I'm guessing the word *vomit* will be used in her response.

Through years of breaking ourselves open and pouring ourselves out for our children, we are awakened, sometimes painfully so, to their very real and eternal presence within our own hearts and souls. Within a healthy family dynamic, we give them roots, we give them wings, and we become vulnerably aware that there is no point in space or in spirit where our lives stop and their lives start. There is no existential gap between us and them, only an awakening to oneness.

As we grow in age and wisdom, we see this working in the other generational direction as well. We become aware that we are embodied within our parents and they within us, even as we invested our rebellious years trying to deny or dissolve this reality. When we sit with aging parents, especially those surrendering to debilitating diseases, we see our own struggles, pains, joys, and triumphs in their vulnerability, fragility, and compromised dignity. If we are spiritually awake, we recognize that their journey and our journey are eternally entwined. It's as though the last dying gift they give us is a keen awareness of how much they live in us, and we die with them. Finally, we see a life raised up from the elements of the earth, broken open, poured out, and shared with us. Their life is our life—one in flesh and blood, one in heart and mind, one in soul and spirit. It's a very holy communion indeed! *Do this* in memory of me.

Amazingly, we don't just have this experience with our parents and children. We also enter into it with spouses, siblings, and close friends. To a greater or lesser degree, we have it with anyone with whom we have lived in real presence, anyone whom we have let love us in our brokenness—and we in theirs.

If you're tracking with me, you already see where this is headed. As we live more deeply in real presence, our spirituality ripples into an ever-widening holy communion with all God's people. At a relatively rudimentary level, we see only our individual relationship with God. We acknowledge that other people also have relationships with God, but we don't connect them with our own. At this level, we say things like, "I'm just here to get my Eucharist" because that's how we see and understand. Life's still mostly about us, and the flow of love's energy in our life is outside-in. Eucharist, the Body of Christ, is seen as a life-giving object we receive. This is the level at which we understand when we're in second grade and we make our first Communion.

As we grow deeper in spirituality, we realize it's not all about us. There are these other people we care about, other people we love, and these people are all created in the image and likeness of God as well. These are our family members and close friends, our "tribe" if you will, the people for whom we would literally give our lives. They reveal to us the miracle of shared love, the reality of life-giving love. If these relationships are healthy, they offer a mutuality through which we discover what it means to be in communion with others, to break ourselves open and pour ourselves out for the welfare of another person. These relationships show us that God's love does not only flow to us; it also flows through us.

Still, however, at this level of spiritual understanding, we see through the polarizing lens of "us and them." Those who are part of our close community or tribe are in the "us" set, and those who are outside of that circle are in the "them" set. *Love of neighbor* is quickly reduced to love of those in the "us" group juxtaposed by animosity or fear of those in the "them" group. The typical Christian response of those who are mired at this level of spiritual development is to go forth and try to make *them* more like *us.*

Looking at the way Jesus lived his life, especially his open engagement with so many people who were very unlike him, it's difficult to imagine that this is what he envisioned when he instituted Eucharist and said, "Do this in memory of me."

The first three ripples of relationship are relatively easy. We are motivated with self-interest to love God, self, and those with whom we are in close relationship. But living in loving communion with total strangers, especially those body-pierced, purple-haired, skateboard punks outside my window...well, let's just say it would be so much easier to love them if they would pull their pants up, stand up straight, and be more like me. Oops. That sure happened quickly.

Living in loving relationship with society, with community—that might be the hardest part of being Christian. In this regard, Eucharist is a tremendous gift. But we have to enter into it fully. I mean really enter into it, not just scrape over the surface and think we're somehow righteous because we go to Mass once a week and hang a rosary from the mirror in the car.

This brings us into the next inner depth of spirituality: living in real presence with the sacred human dignity of every other person, including those who are not at all like us. The good Samaritan parable is a great example of how Jesus felt about this. The story's hero is a man of a different ethnic identity and a different religion. In many ways, he would have been considered an enemy. And we are left with a poignant answer to the question, "Who is my neighbor?" The answer, of course, is everyone. Everyone. Every leper, prostitute, tax collector, Pharisee, refugee, Vikings fan, Democrat, NRA member, tree-hugger, Muslim, immigrant, Republican, and Kardashian. Every single one. Jesus sought to be in communion with them all, and he never once said, "I will love you once you pull your pants up and stand up straight." Do *we*?

I was watching some kids do tricks on their skateboards outside my window. They were different from me is so many, many ways. At first, I was annoyed by the noise they were making. Then I was offended by the language they were using. But I kept watching. Some were brilliantly talented and truly entertaining. I began noticing their giftedness. Then I noticed something else—they really encouraged each other. These guys were of different skill levels, but the more advanced kids did not act entitled at all. They made sure every other kid got time and space to develop and practice his skill. And when someone made an error, they didn't tease or berate; they encouraged and supported. At one point, a young man whom I'd guess to be about fourteen took a nasty digger and face-planted on the boardwalk. At first, it looked as though he might be seriously injured. These kids all hopped off their boards and ran to him. They were genuinely concerned, and it was obvious they cared deeply. I suddenly realized these were young men who authentically loved each other and brought real presence to one another. Why didn't I see that first? Why was my first impression negative? That's not about them; that's about me.

It's worthwhile to go back and revisit the penitential rite and its role in a celebration of Eucharist. One of the very first things Catholics do when we gather in community is acknowledge that we're not so hot ourselves. We publicly acknowledge we're pilgrims on a journey who have not yet arrived. We're still messing up, having uncharitable thoughts, saying unloving things, and making decisions we're not proud of. This simple expression puts us on a level field. We're essentially saying to God, self, and one another, "Look, I'm not perfect. I have no right to judge anyone. Thank you, God, for loving me anyway." It's an exercise in real presence with one another. We shed our pretenses and bare our authentic selves.

When we struggle to love others because they're of a different disposition, affiliation, orientation, heritage, tradition, or generation, Eucharist challenges us to acknowledge that we're not exactly worthy ourselves. And, by the way, they're part of the body of Christ too. If we're truly honest with ourselves, we'll recognize that the real issue is that we find their brokenness more objectionable than we find our own. Such silliness. It turns out the real inhibitor to our love isn't the other person at all; it's our own arrogance and insecurity.

Eucharist invites us to experience a life that leaves all such nonsense behind, a life where we enter into real presence with one another, even those who will deny us and betray us. Feed the hungry. Give drink to the thirsty. Care for the sick. Love your enemy. Break yourself open. Pour yourself out. Let the love in your life flow from the inside-out. *Do this* in memory of me.

Real Presence in Our Relationship with Creation

You can't lie to the trees. Lord knows I've tried. We all have at times, I imagine. Who among us hasn't edited, filtered, and retold their own story into the listening ear of forest, horizon, or night sky? We might not speak it aloud, but we certainly frame it in our minds, recasting our faults, heralding our virtues, and waiting for nature to agree with our self-created version of who we are. But you can't lie to the trees. The wind blows our self-deceptions back in our face. Creation knows who we really are because it is made of all the same stuff we are. And frankly, it already sees the image and likeness of the Creator expressed in us. No, nature doesn't need to be convinced of our authentic self, our real presence; we do.

The clay of the earth—the very same stuff we're made of—doesn't care about our images and pretenses. It doesn't care about the brands on our handbags or the sizes of our homes. It doesn't care about the balance in our checkbooks, the degrees on our walls, or the posts on our social media accounts. The earth under our feet, the sun on our shoulders, the wind in our lungs, the water we drink, and the foods we eat—everything that sustains the very essence of our lives—none of it cares about any of the contrivances we hide behind and spend our days worrying about. Not even a little. Not at all.

No wonder God looked upon everything once it was created and said, "This is very good." Indeed, it is.

No wonder whenever Jesus wanted to recenter and reconnect with God, he went to the wilderness—to the mountains, to the desert, to the sea, to the garden. He did not go to the couch for a Netflix binge, or to a medispa for a cucumber facial, or to Amazon for retail therapy, or to the back of his mind to rehash old conversations. He went to creation, to nature. This is where wholeness, oneness, complete unity with Creator and all creation flows through us. Eucharist, taken from the grain of wheat fallen to the ground and the grape plucked from the vine, brings the real presence of God's creation into oneness within us. It's beautiful.

God's creation has a patient way of silently receiving our thoughts, ponderings, complaints, objections, hopes, dreams, all of everything stirring around in our heads. It draws all this goop out of us until our heads are emptied and we speak from our hearts. Then it listens to our hearts until they too have been laid bare. Finally, once we're emptied of all our swirls, whirls, prejudices, and passions, we speak only the truth from our souls. This is who we really are. Once emptied, we listen as the life-breath of

Spirit breathes the Creator's love—the Body and Blood of Christ—into our lungs, into our own blood, bringing calm to our hearts and peace to our minds. Here we find harmony and wholeness.

Whether intentionally or coincidentally, this is the same contemplative journey the Catholic Mass follows, or at least ought to. We first empty our heads and hearts in an admission of the thoughts, words, and actions that cause suffering for ourselves and others. Then we open ourselves to the word of God proclaimed on the winds of breath. Finally, we are filled with the very nature of Christ. Ultimately, we become one in Christ as Christ is one in the Creator.

Again, my apologies for getting all churchy there, but I fear we've lost sight of the reality that what happens in church and what happens in life are not different things at all. I fear we've lost our deep appreciation for the Eucharist not because we've lost faith, but because we've lost the willingness to empty ourselves and open ourselves. We've lost the humility to admit our brokenness, and the strength to stand vulnerably without the ego protection of image and personality. Eucharist calls us back to our authentic selves, our real presence, which just so happens to have been created in God's image.

While I prefer to retreat to the lush richness of the forest or the quiet vistas of the mountains. Michelle will occasionally lure me into a hike in the desert. This is a very different experience. With no trees, no canopy, the reality of my vulnerability rockets to anxiety level as soon as I get beyond sight of my car. The initial temptation to walk fifty yards, turn around, and call it a day has a powerful attraction. Why on earth would I want to walk farther away from shade, farther away from water, and farther away from the twin miracles of cold beer and pizza delivery? The hot sun, the parched earth, and the unseen dangers of rattlesnakes and scorpions take a neon highlighter to the fragile reality of human life. No thank you, my brain says. Ahh, but yes please, my soul calls. So I journey on, but at a much slower pace than Michelle. Soon I lose sight even of her.

After about two miles, the anxiety burns itself out like a cheap candle. Alone with God in the emptiness of a desert, life's stresses, pressures, doubts, and falsehoods are vacuumed out of me. I awaken to the realization that the sky is real, the earth is real, and love is real. Everything else is exposed as illusion. Deeper into the peace of nothingness, I finally emerge into the fullness of all-ness.

Peace be with you, Jesus said when he entered the upper room. Peace be with you we say before sharing Eucharist. The peace of real presence—this is where we find our holy communion, our sacred unity with God, neighbor, and all creation now and forever.

When we are able to live in communion with God, with self, with others, with society, and ultimately with all of creation, we are able to live in peace, harmony, and love. The gift of Eucharist opens our eyes and our hearts to this reality, not only as a future heaven, but as the real presence on earth as it is in heaven. Jesus, of course, understood this. He also understood that this holy communion is not something we can know intellectually, it is something we are blessed to engage experientially.

Do this in memory of me.

AT THE CLOSE, OPENING

I f someone had told the twenty-one-year-old me that I would become a spiritual author and one day write the book you're holding in your hands, I would have wondered what they had stirred into their coffee. Seriously, I would have thought they were a remarkably poor judge of human character, clearly disengaged from reality. Yet here we are. Funny how God works.

None of this was in my vision for my life. My notion was to use my talents to become a political satirist. I imagined myself writing witty books and columns that laid bare the truth about human society in a way people could no longer deny or ignore. This is how I would help humanity grow toward harmonic unity with one another. Yeah, I was ridiculously naïve.

Also, however, I was keenly aware that I oughtn't be in charge of my own life. I mean, goodness, I was the type of guy who wore a Bart Simpson t-shirt that said "Don't have a cow" to the birth of his own child. A guy like that shouldn't try to run his own show. My only saving grace was in recognizing this about myself. So, I agreed to a very sincere arrangement with God—God runs the show and I do the grunt work. God leads and I follow. Not surprisingly, God chose to lead me down a path other than political satire. For this, I am grateful.

Eventually, I grew to understand and appreciate that our Creator has a far greater interest in moving hearts and stirring souls than in making laws. I won't speculate as to the reasons (or the wisdom) for that, but that's how Christ went about his work as well. Jesus gifted us with a much better path to walk toward a life of unity, harmony, peace, and love—Eucharist. We needn't rely on the proceedings of governments and other civil structures to pave humanity's way toward happiness and joy. We can do it ourselves by breaking bread together.

The question I am most often asked by friends and family members who have wandered from their Catholic roots, whether actively or passively, is why do I stay? Their perspective is often coming from a broken heart, a heart that has felt the Christ-like pain of betrayal or rejection. Most often, it's an honest question more than a challenging one. Why do I stay?

The answer is easy and obvious for me: Eucharist. Once we open ourselves to the deeper mystery of real presence, we are able to glimpse the magnificence of the gift. The Body and Blood of Christ is so much more than a physical specimen. It is a soothing balm, a healing salve. It is hope, compassion, and mercy. It is the promise delivered and the potential realized of unity between Creator, creating, and creation. It is love. And it is given to us freely, asking only that we open ourselves to it.

Again and again, I am reminded that I am broken and on a journey toward wholeness. We all are, I suppose. The gift of Eucharist, and the joy of living a eucharistic way of life, brings us into real presence with God, with self, with others, and with all creation. Here we find wholeness. I pray these fruits of my labors, this work of my hands, helps you find a deeper, life-defining engagement with the love of Christ.

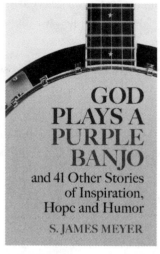
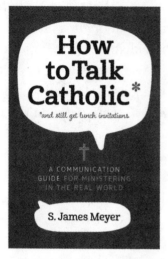

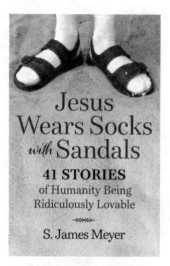